Flowerpot Farming

Creating Your Own
Urban Kitchen Garden

by
Jayne Neville

Published by The Good Life Press Ltd. 2008

ISBN 978 1 90487 131 6
A catalogue record for this book is available from
the British Library.

Published by
The Good Life Press Ltd.
PO Box 536
Preston
PR2 9ZY

www.goodlifepress.co.uk

Photo Credits: Pages 129, 131 Access Garden Products,
Page 130 Paul Peacock

Set by The Good Life Press Ltd.
Printed and bound in Great Britain
by Cromwell Press

Flowerpot Farming
Creating Your Own Urban Kitchen Garden

This book is dedicated to my father, whose passion
for growing vegetables was an inspiration.

By Jayne Neville

Contents

Introduction

If you have ever wanted to grow your own fruit and vegetables but felt you didn't have the space or the expertise, I hope this book will change your mind.

Imagine being able to go out into your own garden today to harvest fresh, tasty, organic seasonal produce you have grown yourself. To be honest, you don't even need a garden: a patio, balcony, roof terrace or even a window box will do just fine. There are really very few vegetables you cannot grow in containers or small spaces so long as you choose the container or use the space with that particular vegetable in mind. Picked straight from the plant, the vegetables you can grow are guaranteed to be better than anything you will ever buy from the shops because i) you grew them yourself, ii) they will be the freshest you will ever taste - reaching your kitchen in a matter of seconds, iii) you know exactly what went into growing them, and last but not least, iv) the big sense of achievement you will get from growing them yourself. Nothing beats the thrill of harvesting

Flowerpot Farming

your own produce whether it's the first crop you have ever grown or you have been cultivating vegetables for years.

Perhaps you would like to take up the challenge of growing an unusual vegetable or herb that you rarely see in the shops, or a variety you will only ever get to try if you grow it yourself. Now that <u>is</u> an incentive! Have you ever eaten kohl rabi, Jerusalem artichokes, Turk's Turban squash, white radishes, Yellow Pear tomatoes or Chinese red mustard? Or eaten corn on the cob just minutes after it was picked? Sliced a home-grown cucumber, and seen and tasted how fresh it was? These are simply worlds apart from shop-bought vegetables, which even if grown both naturally and locally, will never, ever reach you in such great condition as produce fresh from your own garden.

A trip to any garden centre to look at the selection of seeds on offer will show you how many varieties exist of certain vegetables. And these are only the tip of the iceberg; there are many specialist seed companies that offer an even bigger choice. Take the tomato for example: there are literally hundreds of varieties – but you will be able to count on one hand the very limited range for sale in the shops. You will be able to grow 'mini veg', especially suited for smaller spaces, 'heritage' vegetables for that special taste from the past and even some 'pretty', edible crops that won't look out of place grown in a flower border – combining both beauty and bounty.

If you are a keen cook or simply want to use the freshest ingredients in your recipes, then growing much of it yourself is a great step to take. Not only will you be able to impress people with your culinary expertise – you will be able to tell them that the vegetables were also

grown by you in your own garden!

You will be eating the fruits of your labours when they are actually in season, not when a supermarket has shipped them in from abroad. With a small amount of planning and preparation you should be able to have fresh vegetables ready for harvest during most of the year. The best part of this is that it certainly won't have travelled halfway around the world to reach your plate! A few short steps are the biggest distance your crops will have to travel.

One of the many good things about growing fruit and vegetables in small spaces is that anyone can do it; young or old, able bodied or not so agile, time rich or constantly pushed for time – you can design your mini-vegetable farm to suit you. Containers can be chosen especially for ease of use, for economy, for labour saving or simply because they look attractive on your patio. The plants won't care whether they're in an old bucket or the most expensive container in the garden centre and given the same amount of attention, a great result will come from both. Some of your crops could be perennials, which

Flowerpot Farming

stay in their pots or are planted in the same space for several years, for example apple trees and soft fruit bushes. Others may be in their containers from anything from just a few weeks to a whole growing season, as in the case of lettuces, beetroot and most of the varieties we will be looking at growing in this book.

Don't worry if you have never grown anything in your life; contrary to popular belief – gardening isn't complicated or too exacting. Just by following a few simple rules something will come up. Just because you might have heard a few technical gardening terms, don't let that put you off. In its basic form, growing vegetables really is as easy as you want to make it. Many an expert vegetable grower started from growing easy-to-care-for varieties in small spaces and then went on to bigger and better things – a warning perhaps that when the gardening bug bites it can become addictive!

A few packets of seed, the minimum of tools, some compost, and a couple of containers – that's all you really need to get your own mini-allotment going. Once you have discovered the joy of growing and eating your own garden produce, I'm sure you will want to expand and try to grow even more. One thing is for certain; once you have harvested and tasted just one of your own crops, the fruit and vegetables for sale in the shops will never seem quite the same again. However few (or many) vegetables you're planning in your plot, I hope you have lots of fun growing and eating them. So what are you waiting for - let's get started!

Jayne Neville
2008

Chapter One
Why Grow Your Own?

What are your reasons for wanting to grow your own fruit and vegetables? Is it because you want to eat more healthily, be able to choose from a better selection of vegetables, eat fresher produce, learn how to grow your own food, eat vegetables you know are grown organically, or simply because you want to have more control over what you eat, leading to a better, more fulfilling lifestyle?

Have you been thinking of growing things for ages but have not done so yet because of one or more of the following excuses?

Isn't it time-consuming and hard work?
I don't have 'green fingers'/I haven't got a garden
It will be too expensive/I'm just too busy
My kids don't eat vegetables

Flowerpot Farming

Well, the good news is that all of these situations can be easily overcome.

You can tailor the amount of vegetables you grow to suit yourself. If time is a factor, you can limit the amount you grow to suit the available amount of time you have to spare. If this means you want to grow just a few lettuces in a container then that's fine. They will definitely be the best lettuces you have ever tried and caring for them right from the moment you sow the very first seed to the final plant you harvest will take very little time and effort on your part. Most of your time, once the seeds have germinated and been planted out, will be spent making sure your vegetables have enough to drink.

If you've never grown anything in your life before, the thought of growing something that will be good to eat may be daunting, especially as many of us in towns lost our links with the countryside and farming generations ago. Buying carrots or apples from the supermarket may seem a world away from producing something like that yourself, but believe me, you are only a few simple steps away from doing just that.

If your garden is very small, paved over or even non-existent, it is not an obstacle to producing an abundance of fresh vegetables for your dinner table on a daily basis. A very small garden can be adapted, edible plants can be trained up walls, over sheds and vegetables grown in amongst any existing plants in the border. Some vegetable plants are quite beautiful in their own right – take for example the colourful varieties of Swiss chard, or the deep maroon leaves of beetroot. For an architectural statement in a border, a single globe artichoke with its large silver serrated leaves is hard to beat.

Patios and courtyards are excellent places for growing

fruit and vegetables, as long as they are not constantly shaded from the sun, and as many pots and containers as you want to squeeze in can be crammed full of home-grown produce.

Window boxes attached to sunny, sheltered windowsills can be really productive, and you can grow anything from herbs to salad leaves and fast growing vegetables like spinach, pak-choi and rocket to name just some. In just a few short weeks you could be harvesting vegetables to be proud of!

A single globe arichoke makes a stunning architectural statement in a border.

Roof gardens, terraces and balconies are more great spaces for food production, and depending on the amount and variety of things you want to grow, can also become mini-allotments. Pots and containers of all sorts can be used to suit your vegetables and your own needs, bearing in mind that weight will be a consideration when planning how much to grow and in particular the containers you will use - the lighter the pots, the more you can grow on your roof or balcony.

In its simplest form 'flowerpot farming' requires very little in the way of initial investment, especially if you are starting small with just a few containers or a limited space in the garden. As with many things, it is up to you to choose as many tools and as much equipment as you think necessary, but it really is possible to start your vegetable growing career off with an outlay of less than ten pounds. This would include a couple of packets of seed and seed trays, a little compost and basic 'budget' hand tools. Once the growing bug has well and truly bitten, you will probably want to invest in better tools and a wider range of equipment.

If you get really keen and inspired by growing your own produce, then the amount of time and effort you spend on your plants on a daily basis will not be an issue – the satisfaction you get by producing something truly delicious and nutritious will be a reward in itself. However, if you have a really busy lifestyle, the amount and type of plants you grow can be tailored to suit the time you have available. There are some vegetable plants that need little care apart from daily watering in the heat of summer and, if you only have a pot or two or a window box, then tending your 'veg plot' will take only a few minutes a day.

For a keen or budding cook how nice it would be to pop out into your garden or to gather from your window box a fresh herb that is called for in the recipe you are preparing! Growing your own vegetables, particularly herbs and the more unusual varieties, will give you access to a wealth of strains now rarely seen in the shops, many of them 'heritage' types which were very popular in the past but that have now fallen out of favour because they respond better to organic growing methods used in earlier times.

As well as instructions for container growing, this book also describes how to grow vegetables outside in the garden (in a dedicated vegetable plot or vegetable/flower border) and in raised beds. Although primarily aimed at those whose garden space is very limited indeed, there are many more who will be lucky enough to be able to choose to grow their vegetables either in containers or in an area in their garden, or indeed both. Who knows, you may even decide to take on an allotment, or move to a house with a garden at some time in the future.

A big bonus of raising some of your own produce is the physical aspect of actually getting out into the fresh air and doing something practical and worthwhile. Not only is it good for your body, but gardening sets you thinking and planning and can be both challenging and relaxing at the same time.

Getting your children involved in raising their own food will also increase the likelihood that they will eat it; well that's the theory! At the very least they will know how it is grown and the effort that goes into producing it. Getting them to start with vegetables they like to eat and others that are fast growing should keep their interest long enough to see the growing process through from start to finish. One day they might even want a vegetable patch of their own!

Chapter Two
Your Plot

You can grow vegetables practically anywhere. Even if you haven't got a garden, fresh produce can be grown in containers, window boxes, on balconies, roof terraces or even up walls. Take heart that even people possessing large gardens or allotments are likely to say that their plots are far from ideal. They may be exposed to strong winds, have poor soil, be in a shaded situation or overshadowed by tall trees or hedges. It is an extremely lucky person who can say their plants are growing in an ideal situation. The majority of us have to make do with what we have, and the best part of that is that practically any problem can be overcome with a bit of thought and effort.

So long as they are situated in a spot which gets some sunshine in the summer, a good variety of vegetables will grow in small spaces. Nowhere is too small not to be able to grow just a little food. Pots can be filled with herbs – even fruit trees can be grown in pots and make nice features on patios and in small courtyard gardens. The first step, once you've decided to try growing some crops of your own, is to take a good look at what your growing space has to offer.

I would venture to say that the soil in your garden is THE most important ingredient for raising your vegetables and fruit successfully once you have safely planted them. So knowing the type of soil you have, its quality and how to improve it, is very important. It can make the difference between getting a mediocre crop or a bumper one. If you are growing in containers or pots, you can skip this bit if you want, but understanding why soil matters, what it does and how to improve it, will come in handy if you move to a house with a garden or take on an allotment in the future. However, don't get too hung up about having a perfect soil – adding a bit of organic matter as explained below will get you off to a flying start – growing vegetables is about having fun too, and shouldn't become a worry or a chore. Enjoy!

The ideal soil is easy to dig and drains well but has enough body to retain both nutrients and moisture. It provides the ideal habitat for useful organisms such as earthworms, fungi, beetles and good bacteria; all beneficial elements that make up great soil.

A simple soil testing kit which you can buy at a garden centre will tell you how acid or alkaline (limey) your soil is. The kit will test the pH level which measures acidity. The ideal level is pH 6.5 for vegetables, but you can add more lime if it is too acidic. This can be bought from a garden centre with instructions for usage displayed on the product. Garden soil can range anywhere between pH 4.5 and pH 7.5. That's the technical bit over with and, although they might sound complicated, soil test kits are really easy to use.

Soil types

Basically, there are five soil types; silt, clay, sand, chalk and peat and knowing which sort you have will indicate how it needs to be cultivated. To find out what type you have, grab a handful of soil and squeeze it in your hand. A clay soil will stick together in a ball and feels smooth. Sand is the opposite and will feel slightly gritty and fall through your fingers instead of its particles holding together. Silt has a silkier feel and will stick together slightly when squeezed but not so much as clay. Although silty soil is always cited as the ideal growing medium, there is much that can be done to improve the other two, and silt will still benefit from the addition of nutrient adding organic matter. Bear in mind that soil types are rarely so 'cut and dried' as this: some clays can be slightly silty and some silts can carry more sand than others, for example. All soils will benefit from having a regular fix of organic matter dug into them at regular intervals. This will improve the structure of a sandy soil by bulking it up and helping to hold in moisture and nutrients more efficiently. Clay soil is improved if some grit is added along with the organic matter to assist with drainage.

The soil in your garden is divided into three layers. The depth of each of these layers will vary from area to area – even from garden to garden, if soil improvements have been made to the soil in one and not another. The first layer, not surprisingly referred to as 'topsoil', is the most important one because, unless they have exceptionally long roots, it is in this layer that your crops will grow. The topsoil is the layer to which we can make big improvements by adding lots of organic matter. The two remaining layers are subsoil and the parent matter layer. Subsoil is lighter in colour than topsoil because it contains no humus and is almost devoid of nutrients. It is because of this that we gardeners always concentrate on building up the topsoil thickness by adding organic matter – the thicker the layer of topsoil, the less likely it is that a plant's roots will come into contact with the subsoil where there is very little in the way of food. The subsoil also affects the water-holding capacity of the soil too, but again, this can be improved somewhat by bulking up the topsoil.

The final layer is simply the bedrock or natural rocky layer, which is normally buried so deep that it shouldn't really affect you at all, unless your garden is on a steep hill, when this layer will be nearer the surface, the two upper layers being much thinner. Again, this situation can be overcome to some extent by adding lots of organic material to the topsoil.

Organic matter

You will see the term 'organic matter' mentioned in numerous gardening books but what is it? Basically, this is any natural material that adds vital nutrients to the soil. This could be well-rotted garden compost, well-rotted farmyard manure, green manures (plants especially grown to be dug into the soil after a specified period to build fertility) or spent mushroom compost. These are best dug in during the autumn before you begin using your plot, but can also be applied as a thick layer of mulch to the soil's surface, when it will eventually be taken down below the surface by earthworms. This surface layer also acts as a good weed suppressant through the year and as a moisture retainer in hot, dry weather.

Flowerpot Farming

Adding more organic matter each autumn after harvest will put back the nutrients the previous crops have taken from the soil. It will then be ready for the next growing season.

Getting hold of animal manure can be difficult if you live in a town, but it might be worth tracking down a local riding school or livery stables who may be more than happy to let you have a few sacks of horse muck. Cow manure is an alternative but is more easily obtained in rural areas.

Some garden centres sell pre-packed sacks of manure alongside sacks of compost and mulch materials. This is a very expensive way of buying it, but if you only require a small amount then it is perhaps better than hunting around for manure 'straight from the field', and it will be ready to use immediately. Fresh manure is best left to compost for several months and any straw mixed in with it will also by then have rotted down too. More commonly these days, horses are bedded on wood shavings, which take a lot longer (usually around one year) to be ready for incorporating into the soil. Never incorporate fresh manure straight into the soil and always make sure that any wood shavings are thoroughly rotted down before using them – wood particles actually take nitrogen from the soil as they decompose, the exact opposite of what we are aiming for! After being left for a year or thereabouts (forking it over occasionally to allow aeration and quick decomposition), the shavings will disappear into a lovely organic matter and will be ready to use. You can of course mix animal manure into your compost bin along with plant material and use it all together. Poultry manure is another good source, but it is very strong and should be mixed into the compost heap where it will then act as an activator. Poultry manure in the form of dried pellets bought from a garden centre is a different thing altogether. This can be sprinkled around growing plants or lightly dug in around them during the growing season as a crop boosting quick release fertiliser.

What soil to use if you are growing in containers

If your vegetable farming is to be done solely in pots and containers then you will probably be buying in compost from elsewhere to fill up your containers and plant your vegetables. Please don't be tempted to use soil straight from someone else's garden – there is a distinct possibility that it will carry disease, but most of all it will most likely be very unbalanced and lacking in many of the nutrients that your plants will require. Do yourself a favour and buy some good quality multi- purpose compost for filling your pots. At least you will know you are starting off your plants in the best way in a good growing medium. You can also add extra organic matter to your bought-in compost at the time of planting and then give the compost an organic boost later by way of poultry pellets or seaweed liquid when the vegetables need the extra food for continued healthy growth. Placing a layer of mulch made from organic matter on the surface of the pots is also beneficial in helping the soil retain moisture for longer.

The small garden

If you are lucky enough to have some outside space available for planting vegetables directly into the soil, then it should be possible to have a go at all of the planting suggestions in this book.

A major concern if you have a very neat town garden

Flowerpot Farming

might be that turning some of it over to vegetable growing will make it look untidy. There is no reason why it should, provided it is kept weeded and tended just like any other part of your garden. It really is quite feasible to have an attractive garden with both flowers and vegetables growing alongside each other, or you could divide the space up for flowers and ornamental plants with another separate area for your vegetables. Front gardens too can provide a bit more space for growing edible crops and, if chosen correctly, your vegetable plants will be as attractive a feature as if you were planting up with annual bedding or perennials. A friend of mine grew a miniature pumpkin in her front garden one year, and the resulting fruits drew attention from all who saw them, especially close to Halloween, when some of the pumpkins were carved in situ still on the plant! The large trailing leaves were arranged around the other plants in the border and looked quite striking.

If you must have a neat front garden, a perennial herb bed is a good choice. Plants like rosemary, bay, thyme, sage and lavender need little maintenance and can all be kept trimmed to a manageable size. Alternatively, a nice big container filled with herbs near the entrance is a great alternative to the annual displays most people have and they will look and smell good for far longer (and can be used to flavour your cooking, of course). A couple of specimen bay trees in pots on either side of a front door would look very impressive and be useful too. There is really no reason why you can't turn the whole of your front garden into a mini-allotment, but this is, I suppose, a step too far for the majority of people!

A dedicated plot in the back garden is, I would guess, most people's idea of the best place for growing vegetables in town. Obviously, the more space you have the better it is if you want to try lots of different varie-

A well thought out herb garden can be as attractive as any flower bed.

ties, and this could be arranged as one large area or be divided up into separate or raised, smaller beds. These are a great idea if you want a low-maintenance kitchen garden as you can separate the beds with paths in between, making it easier to reach the centre of each one without having to tread on the soil too much. This will mean you have to decide what kind of path you would like, but this can become an attractive feature in its own right, as well as letting you harvest vegetables without getting your shoes muddy.

Crop rotation

Of particular importance if you intend to grow vegetables in your mini-allotment year after year is to practice a 'rotation' scheme. If you have ever heard this mentioned and wondered what on earth it meant, I will try to give you a simple explanation. Most vegetables are related to others and can be classified into 'family' groups. The

23

nutrient requirements for each member of that group are very similar and they will normally be susceptible to the same disease and pest problems; other groups will have different nutritional needs and pests and diseases. If members of the same plant family are grown in the same place year after year they will eventually use up all the nutrients they need in that particular piece of soil. Additionally, pests and diseases common to these particular plants will also build up to excessive levels causing the crops grown there to become progressively weaker and less productive each year until they could eventually fail completely.

To avoid this, it is best to 'rotate' the crops by dividing up (by imaginary means or actual defined areas) the plot into separate areas, then growing each plant family in a different area each year The trick is to know which plant is related to which! Some are easy to recognise as relations such the brassica family, consisting of cabbage, cauliflower, broccoli, kale and Brussels sprouts. However, there are a few vegetables you wouldn't think were brassicas, but they are, such as radishes and turnips. The other main vegetable groups are: Alliums (onions and leeks), Legumes (beans and peas) and Umbellifers (carrots, parsnips, celery and parsley). Chapter four gives more details on these groups and the vegetables they include. However, please don't let rotation become a worry; if you do forget to move a plant group one year, you will still get a crop and there is always the following year to get things back on track!

Vegetables in the border

If you have no room for a separate vegetable plot in your back garden then the best option is to choose vegetables you can grow in amongst your existing border plants. Some vegetables can be used as a focal point: runner beans or climbing French beans trained up a tall wigwam support during the summer can add height to a border and provide colourful flowers, a globe artichoke makes a fine central specimen plant and red leaved kales and chards certainly draw the eye. Fast growing nasturtiums are a dual purpose plant, with bright, colourful flowers and leaves that add a peppery bite to your salads. Low growing salad leaves such as the 'Salad Bowl' lettuce varieties could be used as edging – try alternating between the red and green leaved types for colour impact – cutting off just the leaves for eating with the part left in the ground continues to grow, producing yet more tasty leaves in the weeks to come.

Pergolas and arches are good places to grow climbing fruit and vegetables and are ideal if you are pressed for space as they take up very little room. If you have a sunny wall or fence, this would do just as well, provided there is soil at the base for putting your plants (or room for positioning a container). Victorian kitchen gardens used walls in exactly the same way and often tender fruit trees such as peaches and apricots were trained along the brickwork which protected them and retained heat. If you have such a space, it would be a real pity not to use it.

A courtyard or patio garden

Many courtyard gardens also act as 'outdoor rooms' in the warmer months of the year, and how lovely it would be to be able to both grow and eat the produce grown there if your outdoor space doubles up as a dining room in the summer. The lush foliage of both flowering and vegetable plants can provide a most enticing backdrop to a sultry summer's evening entertaining.

Flowerpot Farming

Unless your courtyard is deeply shaded all the time, you should be able to raise lots of worthwhile tasty vegetables in containers. If it is in a sheltered position, so much the better. Climbing and runner beans can form a backdrop against a wall as could a hardy grapevine. You could even create an arbour over a favourite seat by training climbing beans over a frame. Using an old heritage variety such as 'Painted Lady' (first introduced in 1855), you could take advantage of its pretty red and white flowers to create some extra colour. A courgette in a pot will create a striking focal point with its large, spiky leaves and yellow flowers. A yellow fruiting type or one of the round fruited varieties will make a change from the traditional long green courgettes, or you could choose to grow another member of the squash family such as the aptly named 'Turk's Turban'. Autumn fruiting squashes in particular are available in an array of weird and wonderful shaped fruits – most of them excellent for use in the kitchen.

Cordon tomatoes trained up canes or bush varieties in pots are good choices and a sunny position will ensure the fruits ripen quickly. An outdoor cucumber such as 'Outdoor Ridge' could become both a focal and talking point once the fruits begin to form. To train your plants up a fence or wall you could attach a piece of ready made trellis panel or, more simply, by stringing wires across the surface. These will be hidden, of course, once your climbers are in full growth. For a more natural look a willow or hazel fence panel could be used against which to tie your climbers.

If your courtyard is not completely paved and has areas of open soil, then the scope for a yet wider variety of vegetables is even larger. Root crops such as beetroot and carrots are well worth growing for both their culinary use and their attractive foliage. Carrots of course have those well known delicate and feathery leaves we recognise from growing carrot tops as children, but they can get quite tall and they make a good backdrop to lower growing plants. Beetroot is almost worth growing for its leaves alone, never mind the delicious roots! The 'traditional' deep red coloured beet carries dark glossy green leaves with dark red veins but gaining in popularity is the golden beetroot with the same dark green foliage but veined with a deep mustard yellow. It is almost a crime to pick them when the time comes!

At the front, some colourful lettuce and salad leaves in shallower trays will provide the basic ingredients for your summer salads. 'Cut and come again' leaves can be harvested as required and will re-sprout. Look out for varieties such as 'Red and Green Salad Bowl' and the oriental salad leaf 'Mizuna' with its serrated leaves. Traditional lettuces like cos and iceburg can be sown regularly to ensure a continuous crop. Mediterranean herbs such as spicy oregano, basil 'Red Rubine' and golden marjoram will add even more colour and lushness to the scene. A bay tree or a rosemary plant in a terracotta pot can be a permanent feature through the seasons as they are both perennials.

A kitchen garden on your balcony

Vegetables can be squeezed into the smallest of spaces, and relatively speaking, compared to a window box, a balcony has acres of room. Care must be taken, though, not to overload it with very heavy structures or extremely large containers filled with soil. It is always better to site heavier pots close to the structural wall of your building rather than at the front edge of the balcony or in the middle if it is unsupported. It is advisable to check with a professional structural engineer if you are in doubt as to what loads your balcony might support.

Flowerpot Farming

High rise balconies can often be windy places, but there are plenty of vegetables that can tolerate this and you can always devise ways of protecting your crops from the worst of the elements. A strategically fixed trellis panel or structure with gaps in it will help to diffuse the wind and so protect your plants. Make sure it is firmly fixed in place though! You could even train plants up it, making even better use of the space.

To a certain degree, the choice of crops you can grow on your balcony will depend on which aspect it faces. A south-facing balcony will be able to support the biggest range of vegetables and will ensure that heat loving specimens like tomatoes and cucumbers thrive and produce a worthwhile crop (provided they are kept well fertilised and watered too, of course). Top edible plants for a sunny balcony as well as tomatoes and cucumbers are sweet and chilli peppers (choose a mixture of different varieties for a striking array of fruit colours and shapes), strawberries, rainbow chard, miniature fruit trees and bushes in pots and even grapevines that can be trained around the outer edge of the balcony if it is sheltered enough. If you have somewhere to fix them, a couple of hanging baskets with herbs or tumbling varieties of tomatoes will allow you to squeeze in just a few more things on your balcony. A trailing nasturtium is very easy to grow and, planted in a pot on the floor, can be trained along the front of a balcony railing or up a wall. The flowers and leaves are delicious, giving a peppery taste when they are mixed in with other salad leaves as well as providing a colourful floral display outside your window all through the summer.

In comparison, a more shaded, cooler north-facing balcony will only receive a fraction of direct sunshine in the summer. Vegetables that are less dependent on lots of sun for ripening are the best choice here. Things like beans (all kinds), salad leaves, spinach, compact curly kales, oriental mustard 'red giant' (very attractive and sculptural when mature) are just a few of the options.

Another good thing about a balcony vegetable patch is that its close proximity to a water supply means you won't have to be struggling to carry heavy watering cans for long distances, and because you will probably be in your kitchen garden quite often, you will be able to check each plant's progress, ripeness and sort out any pest problems on your vegetables more quickly than most ordinary gardeners.

The ultimate in balcony gardening is that if you site a table and chairs there, you could even lean across and pick some of your own produce whilst dining. Then food miles are reduced to just centimetrcs!

A vegetable garden inside or outside a window

As well as using a window box attached underneath an outside window, which should be treated in a very similar way to growing crops on a balcony but on a much smaller scale, you can even grow an array of edible crops inside your home on a windowsill. The obvious choices are herbs which can be grown in small pots. Parsley, coriander, basil, oregano, lemon grass and many other favourites will do well inside, as long as they are given enough light. They will bring a touch of the outside world into your kitchen or whatever room is best placed for a light aspect. A really warm spot will make possible the growing of sun loving plants such as chillies and dwarf varieties of tomato. Leafy salads will thrive in smallish trays so long as they are well drained, as their roots are fairly shallow. Quick growing oriental vegetables fall into the same category.

Sprouting seeds such as mung beans, alfalfa and mustard and cress are even more undemanding and don't even need any soil to grow. Purpose made sprouting seed kits and the seeds themselves are readily available or you can simply sow them onto damp kitchen paper and keep them moist. For the small space gardener in a hurry, these are ideal, most being ready to eat in just a few days.

Windowsills are great places for raising young plants from seed, whether or not you plan to keep them indoors once they have germinated. If you don't have a greenhouse then a light, warmish windowsill indoors can be almost as good, if not better than an unheated greenhouse in early spring when there is still a risk of frost. Half-size seed trays usually fit very nicely on a windowsill and, once the seeds are sown into moist compost and covered with clear polythene (or a clear plastic bag), it shouldn't take too long for the young seedlings to make an appearance.

If you live on a ground floor then a window box is another useful space for raising a few more vegetables. If window access is easy, then it could be possible to fit a window box to a higher window, but for safety's sake it must be fixed firmly in place and be able to take the weight of the plants and the compost which can be substantial, particularly after watering.

As with gardening on a balcony, the aspect of the window chosen is important and will dictate which plants will grow best. An assortment of colourful, low growing vegetables would be ideal, but if you wanted to screen a window from the outside world, you could choose to plant taller vegetables, or even frame a window by training trailing or climbing plants around it! Like any form of container, window boxes do dry out quickly, especially in the summer. Be prepared for frequent, heavy watering in hot spells and especially when fruit is forming. Some composts contain gels which hold water longer and may be an option to save on such frequent watering. Don't just think of the window box as a container just for use in the warmer months, though. Hardy vegetables such as perpetual spinach, winter cabbages and lettuce can all survive the winter outside.

When choosing your window box do bear in mind the weight of the box itself, even before it is planted up. Plastic ones are obviously lighter, but perhaps less attractive, whilst sturdy wooden ones and those made of terracotta will be much more weighty. Using a lightweight compost will help to reduce this. Alternatively, you can mix in a few handfuls of Perlite into a standard multi-purpose compost. Perlite is made from volcanic rock, weighs very little and will balance the mixture of air and water in the compost, stopping the soil becoming waterlogged.

A vegetable plot on the roof

An area on a roof offers a great deal of scope, particularly if it is a big one, but you must consider if the roof can structurally take the weight of a garden grown in pots and containers. How high up your roof is will have a bearing on what you can grow and the best way to grow it. Wherever it is you might want to create some shading during the summer to prevent your plants scorching up under the summer sun and will definitely need to provide wind breaks and screening all year round to protect them from the strong winds. It might be that the roof space has a wall around the perimeter or walls within its area which you can use to the benefit of your plants.

Flowerpot Farming

Unless the building itself is nestling amongst other, taller buildings, it is likely that light levels will definitely not be a problem here – there should be plenty of light and plenty of weather too!

A fundamental need is a water supply; particularly if access to your roof is difficult. The exposed position of any roof means that soil will dry out quicker because of both the wind and, in the summer, the sun, too. The larger your repertoire of plants, the more water you will need. If it is possible, a green way of getting water for your plants could be to collect rainwater from the roof gutters, but this could be tricky as you will have to fix rain collectors to the walls under the gutters and then work out a way of getting to it. Less environmentally friendly is to have an outside tap fitted on the roof space but perhaps the easiest in terms of cost to the pocket and time is to simply run a hose from a tap further down inside the building.

Windbreaks can take the form of trellis, as used on a balcony, or any type of design which allows air to pass through, thus lessening the strength of the wind. Whatever windbreak you decide to use, make sure it is extremely well secured. Creating shading on a roof space is quite tricky and, when the sun is overhead, becomes almost impossible, but using taller, more heat tolerant plants to protect smaller, delicate ones will help. At certain times of the day the windbreak trellis panels will also provide shelter from the sun and plants nearby will get the benefit. If your roof will take the weight, you could also site several small fruit trees in containers to provide an attractive screen.

A handsome and now fairly common 'flooring' used on roof gardens is timber decking which gives a natural feel and contrasts nicely with the colours and textures of the plants you will soon have growing up there. It covers unsightly roof surfaces but can also act as a load-bearing device, spreading the weight of containers and structures across a much larger area. Having a roof garden means that you really can spend hours up there, pottering around amongst your vegetables and, after a busy gardening session, relax in a chair amongst the plants.

As with any vegetable garden, time spent in the early stages of planning is time well spent. The practicalities and challenges of getting all the aspects of a roof garden developed might seem rather a chore, but once they are sorted out all that is left to do is the fun part – the actual process of growing those lovely vegetables!

The choice of vegetables to grow on a roof space is wide, so long as you have the right size containers for each one and take into account the best position for them on your roof. Fruit trees are a good choice and can create the most marvellous focal points and add height to any planting schemes; the best ones for roof top growing are apples and pears, both of which can tolerate fluctuating temperatures. Choose a dwarfing rootstock (M27 or M9 for apples or Quince C for pears) – with regular pruning this will ensure that your trees stay a manageable size! The beauty of including trees in your scheme is that they can become permanent fixtures, requiring little more than pruning, replenishing the compost and adding well rotted manure to the pot each autumn. If the tree is a young one, it will need potting up into a larger size as it grows.

You will need to protect your trees in winter, however, particularly as the roots are very vulnerable to the cold when grown in containers. If you haven't anywhere sheltered to bring them into over the coldest months,

Flowerpot Farming

then there are steps you can take to make conditions easier for them. This can be done by bringing them over to a slightly more protected area of the roof and wrapping a thick layer of bubble wrap, fleece or any similar insulating material around the pot.

Herbs, especially ones originating from the Mediterranean, will do well on a roof in a good summer if they are exposed to lots of sunlight. All types of basil (sweet, bush, red, cinnamon, etc.), lemon balm, oregano, summer savoury, thyme: in fact, most herbs are suited to growing outside on a roof. Tomatoes and chillis will also benefit and their fruits will ripen much quicker than their shaded counterparts. Recommended outdoor tomato varieties are given in Chapter 4, but anything from the very tiny 'Totem' to the standard height cordon variety 'Tigerella' (red and orange striped fruits) grow well in pots or grow bags.

Look out for cucumbers especially suited to outdoor conditions such as the ridge variety 'Bush Champion' F1 – a very compact plant and great for container growing. 'Marketmore' is a good choice for training up a small wigwam support or trellis.

French beans are easy to grow in pots from mid-spring onwards, with compact varieties such as the pencil podded variety 'Ferrari' giving excellent yields and 'Purple Queen' with its distinctive coloured pods. An earlier bean for you to grow on your roof is the broad bean 'The Sutton'. It is recommended for windy sites and is a dwarf variety that only reaches 45cm.

All types of squash, courgette, pumpkin and in particular the cobnut squash, which takes a long time to ripen (or sometimes does not do so at all) if grown in a cool shady area, will benefit from a sunny position on a roof.

Sweetcorn needs a good hot summer in order to produce the very largest, mouth-watering cobs, but grouped in a block formation (more on this in the vegetable chapter) there is no reason why you can't get a similar result on your roof in a good season. Onions like an open site with good drainage, so will do very well. Spring onions can be sown in containers outside from early spring to midsummer, and sowing some seed every 4 weeks will guarantee a continual supply. Garlic too will give a good crop as long as you keep the plants well watered.

If your roof is still pretty windswept, then stick with hardier vegetables. Curly kale, particularly the dwarf varieties, are a good choice as is Swiss chard and its relation, perpetual spinach. Cabbages which are, of course, low growing will not be affected by the wind and the underrated kohl rabi, another member of the brassica family, is worth growing for its novelty value alone. In long, low troughs lettuces and other salad leaves will thrive, as will the tasty rocket, which is ideal for growing in pots. Grow the wild variety which does not bolt as quickly as the cultivated varieties such as 'salad rocket'.

Chapter Three
Tools and Equipment for the Job.

The beauty of small-scale fruit and vegetable growing is that you don't need too many tools to begin with. However, if you are completely new to gardening and don't quite know what you will need in the way of tools, it is tempting to buy lots of nice shiny tools 'just in case'; whether or not you will need some of them is another matter. If you are growing completely in containers or in a window box then all that will be required to start with are a few hand tools: a trowel, hand fork, dibber, a pair of gardening gloves and a watering can.

To start your vegetables off from seed you'll also need some seed trays, or you can re-use some of those shallow plastic punnets you get at the supermarket when buying new potatoes, tomatoes, etc. Look after these trays well, because soon you won't be buying many vegetables at the shops! Just make sure they have drainage holes at the bottom to let the moisture out, then your seeds and plants won't risk getting waterlogged and rotten. You will also need some plant labels to mark your seed trays once the seed has been sown into them. If you are growing several different things at once it's easy to forget where you sowed what. After a while you will get to recognise the young seedlings soon after they emerge, but labelling is still useful as some seeds take longer to germinate than others and if you know what is under the soil surface you are less likely to panic.

Trowel

You'll certainly need a trowel for digging in the compost, filling up pots and trays, transplanting seedlings and more, so it's best to get a decent one with a comfortable handle because this is the tool you will probably use the most if you are growing mainly in containers. It will get a lot of use even if you are going to use raised beds or borders for growing your vegetables, particularly for transplanting from seed trays into the beds.

A good trowel will last for many years if you look after it. There are different designs to choose from, the most common being the standard width trowel which you can use for most jobs. These are widely available and you can probably pick one up for as little as £1.00, but it is better to spend a little more to get a better quality trowel that will stand the test of time. To see a wide range of these and other gardening tools, go to a good garden centre. They will have all the tools you need on display and you can compare different ones. Stainless steel is a good bet as it lasts a very long time, is very strong, looks good because it is nice and shiny and is very easy to clean because the soil is less likely to stick to it.

You could also invest in a narrow trowel, which is good for working in confined spaces (so ideal for containers and pots). If you are planting closely, you are less likely to disturb the surrounding plants with this tool. Narrow trowels are also useful for planting bulbs, and many have a graduated measuring gauge imprinted into the metal indicating the depth you can plant.

Hand fork

A hand fork is useful for turning and aerating the soil and rooting out small weeds. You could probably get away with not having one at all, but many are sold in pairs together with a trowel. Most of the points above for choosing trowels apply here too.

Dibber

A dibber can be used for planting larger seeds such as beans which need to be sown at a deeper depth than small seeds (Chapter 4 will tell you all you need to know about seed sowing), and can be used for getting rid of the odd weed, especially in seed trays. They are good for transplanting young plants from seed trays to larger pots, especially for gently teasing seedlings out of module trays. If you are going to use it for sowing, then get a dibber with a measuring guide printed on the side of it. You could make one yourself using a thin piece of wood which tapers at one end and mark the centimetres/inches on it yourself, or you could simply use your finger!

Soil sieve

A sieve is often recommended to sift the soil so it is fine enough to cover over small, delicate seeds on the surface of a seed tray. Large seeds such as beans, peas, squash and beetroot will not need such delicate treatment, but fine seed like lettuce and carrots will find it a struggle to fight their way up to the surface if bulky lumps of compost impede their progress. If you have only small amounts to sow then breaking up the compost with your fingers to get a fine consistency should be fine.

Gardening gloves

You might need some gloves when you are handling compost if you don't like getting your hands dirty, but personally I find it less restricting if I can feel what I am doing when gardening. A pair of rubber washing up gloves might be better for light work if you must wear something on your hands, but when handling tiny seeds and transplanting seedlings, the naked hand really is best!

For more tough work, for example pruning back soft fruit bushes, a pair of leather gloves with reinforced palms are the best. Try to get a pair that fits well; gloves that are too large make gardening really difficult. And don't leave them outside to get wet; once the leather dries out again, the gloves will be too stiff to move your fingers properly.

Notebook

Even if you are only planning on growing a few varieties of vegetables to begin with, it's a really good idea to jot down what you sowed, when you sowed it and where and in what it was sown because, when you come to do the same next year, you will probably have forgotten - or is that just me! A written record is not only useful to see what you need to do next time you are growing the same vegetables, but also if you did have a disaster and one particular crop failed, it will help you to work out why it went wrong and learn from your mistakes. Notes of what sort of yields you get are also interesting to keep and then you can try to better your harvests each year.

It's nice to keep a record of which varieties of vegetables you grew to look back on in future; you will always have your own personal favourites but, after growing different things for a couple of years or so, it's easy to forget which you enjoyed eating and which you didn't.

A notebook can also contain diagrams and information on crop rotation if you are growing your food in garden beds. A small drawing will help you to remember what went where the previous year. If you give your plants liquid feeds then write that down too and when you applied them, so that when you are aiming for another bumper crop the following year, you will know exactly how you achieved the last one. A small pocket sized notebook is probably best as you can carry it around with you noting things down as you are outside with your plants.

Watering can and/or hose

The watering can is a really important part of your equipment as it will be used more than any other item in your gardening kit. The most important thing is to choose one with a fine rose (tiny holes which make the water spray finely rather than pour) – most seeds except the very largest ones need very gentle watering, not a deluge which will certainly displace them, if not wash them away. Alternatively, a hose with a fine spray nozzle will get the job done quicker if you have lots of pots and will prove its worth during the summer months, but you will need an outside tap to connect the hosepipe

Tools and Equipment

to. Some plastic watering cans come with a couple of different sized nozzles, and galvanised cans normally have a screw fitting so you can attach different sized roses to them.

A can that can hold a reasonable volume of water (1-2 gallons) is a good size so you don't have to keep refilling it quite so much. Choosing a can with this capacity means you could go for a traditional galvanised steel one or a much lighter plastic one. Plastic won't last as long, but if you have problems lifting or just want a can that is lightweight to begin with and cheaper too, this might be a good choice for you. A galvanised can, of course, will last you a lifetime.

In these days of global warming and water shortages, it is also wise to invest in a water butt to collect rainwater, which in any case is much better for your plants than tap water.

You might want to consider using 'grey' water (from the bath or shower so use only biodegradable soaps and shampoos) in your garden for washing out pots and for watering some plants that are not directly for eating – trees for example. However, this water should be used extremely sparingly on any plant because eventually additives can build up in the soil, making it unbalanced and withholding nutrients. In containers this result happens even more quickly. Grey water from the kitchen sink will also hold grease and bacteria and should never be used on your plants or on the soil. The Centre for Alternative Technology has advice on its website about making the best use of grey water in the garden.

Another watering solution, particularly for patio/balcony pots in the summer, is a drip kit. This is connected to a hosepipe so you will need an outside tap. A drip kit

Flowerpot Farming

consists of a central tube with smaller tubes coming off it at different intervals. Small nozzles are fitted at the end of each of the smaller tubes and these dispense small amounts of water. These are particularly useful if you are going on holiday or are out at work all day during the summer. The individual tubes are fixed onto each pot or container that needs watering and a slow supply of water is dispensed when the mains supply is turned on. The higher specification kits also come with a timer switch that can be set to come on at required intervals. This method is much less wasteful than using a hosepipe because the water is directed exactly where it is needed.

Another similar option for use on a raised bed or outside soil surface is a 'seep hose', or porous pipe, arranged around the plants that need watering. The water goes straight to the roots of the vegetables and there is no wasteful evaporation as there is with overhead watering.

Pruners/secateurs

If you are thinking of growing soft fruit or tree fruit in pots or out in your garden, then you will need a good pair of secateurs for pruning the plants back during the winter and generally keeping them in trim throughout the rest of the year. There are two main types to choose from: bypass and anvil – which describe their cutting actions. Bypass secateurs are best for cutting softer stems or new growth and produce a cleaner cut and the anvil type are more suited to cutting hard, woody growth when they are less likely to jam. Some of the specialist companies have styles for left-handers and people with smaller hands. It really is worth going along to a good garden centre to see a selection and try them for size. As always, some are more expensive than others but they will last the longest and are likely to be more comfortable to use. It really depends on how much pruning you will be doing and how far your budget will stretch.

Tools for raised beds/borders/ larger plots

Larger vegetable beds will definitely require a garden fork for soil preparation and perhaps a spade for incorporating compost and organic matter. Digging spades and forks are available in two sizes: general purpose ones which tend to be on the large size, and a slightly smaller version called a border fork or spade. To my mind the border versions are better suited to smaller scale plots, and much easier to use if you are of smaller stature.

My most important tool during the growing season is a hoe, preferably a long-handled one, but if your vegetable bed is reasonably compact, a small hand hoe (sometimes called an onion hoe) should be able to do the job quite adequately. Hoeing around your vegetables in the summer to keep the plot weed free is one of the most important jobs in the garden because it stops the weeds competing with your precious veg! Your crops will always grow bigger and healthier if they are not struggling to compete with other plants.

Flowerpot Farming

A rake is useful if you are sowing seed directly into your outdoor beds and need a level soil surface with a nice fine 'tilth' to sow your seed into. Tiny seeds especially need sowing either just below or on the surface of the soil, and clods of earth will definitely impede their chances of coming up.

An important task every time you use your tools is to clean them afterwards. As well as keeping them ready for the next time you use them, keeping them clean will prolong their life and just as importantly will prevent the possible spread of disease from one plant to another. If the handles are made of wood, oiling them with natural oils such as linseed or teak keeps the wood waterproofed, nourished, shiny, smooth and pleasant to handle.

Storing your tools

If you are solely gardening in containers and are only going to be using hand tools, this won't be an issue as your gardening kit will be small enough to be kept indoors but, for bigger tools like spades, forks, and hoes it's best to have somewhere secure where they can all be kept together. Small garden sheds could be an option if you have the space in your garden to put them. There are many different sizes to choose from – some of the smallest I have seen look like small sentry boxes which would do just fine for hanging up tools and rolls of hosepipe, and would fit into the corner of a small backyard. It needn't be an eyesore either; with some French climbing beans trained over it in the summer you would hardly know it was there. If, however, you don't have the room or don't want a shed in your garden space, then a garden store could be the answer. This takes the form of a storage chest and can fit neatly against a wall or fence. An added bonus is that you could use it as a seat; sited appropriately you could take a well

earned rest on it at the end of a busy gardening day to admire the fruits of your labour!

Once the vegetable growing bug has bitten, as I am sure it will from the moment you taste your first crop, you will probably want to invest in more tools, and there are certainly lots more to choose from. By then, of course, you will have a good idea exactly what you need and will be less likely to splash out on something that looks good but which you may never use.

The most important tip for tools is to remember where you put them and keep them clean. Treated well good-quality tools can last a lifetime.

Other tools worth considering:

Purpose-made line and reel for sowing seed in straight rows (or you could easily make your own using a couple of short bamboo canes and thin nylon twine).

A long-handled cultivator for aerating the soil – to save your back!

An old, galvanished bucket makes an attractive container.

Containers and pots

There is such a wide choice of pots available today that it could be easy to get carried away and spend a lot of money without ever finding out whether they are really suitable for growing the vegetables you want. Size and shape are both important considerations and more specific guidelines for choosing ideal containers for different types of vegetables are given in Chapter Four on 'How to Grow'.

As well as buying new containers, though, you might want to consider obtaining second hand ones or choosing something more unusual. The plus side of buying new containers is that they will be perfect and suitable for the purpose of growing plants. You will also have a wide choice of shapes and sizes to fit in with what you will be growing. Whatever you decide on, ensure that drainage holes are already present or that you can make some drainage holes in the bottom of the pots yourself.

Buying new pots is the most expensive option, and is great if you want a co-ordinated look in a smart courtyard garden, but if you are looking for something a bit different or are on a budget then second-hand, recycled or unusual items such as old galvanised buckets and troughs, half barrels, stone sinks (probably expensive!), troughs or even an old pair of Wellington boots could be just what you need. Container vegetable gardening should be fun as well as productive and by re-using things you take a step up the sustainability ladder too.

A big advantage of growing herbs in pots is that you can convienently place them where they are handy for instant picking

Terracotta or clay pots are a good choice and not surprisingly have been the gardener's favourite for many years. They are heavy when filled with soil which means they won't topple over at the slightest thing and clay actually keeps the soil warmer than other materials such as plastic or wood, heat being lost much more slowly from clay pots so tender plants don't receive such a check to their growth, particularly in spring. When buying terracotta check that the pots are frost-proof; most modern ones are and then you will be able to use them all year round. Clay is biodegradable will eventually disintegrate if broken into small pieces and dug into the soil. Large shards are useful to use in the bottom of other containers as 'crocks' to help drainage. Do bear in mind that clay pots are porous and therefore tend to dry out a lot quicker than other materials, so be prepared for more frequent watering in the summer. Clay looks lovely when it has weathered a

Flowerpot Farming

bit and will blend in to suit almost any situation. Old clay chimney pots make great features in their own right and their length makes them suitable for growing tapering root vegetables. You should still be able to pick them up relatively cheaply from salvage yards.

Stoneware pots and containers are heavier and more durable but will obviously be more awkward to move around. They hold moisture in the soil more readily, but their weight makes them difficult to move around and not such a good choice on a roof terrace or balcony where load bearing capacities may be an issue. Salvage yards and local auctions are good hunting grounds for old stoneware sinks, which make lovely herb gardens. Although old sinks are very desirable and are often installed in modern homes, the ones that fetch high prices are usually in perfect condition. If you are looking for one to use for planting, then a few chips and slight cracks will bring the price down considerably, and once the sink has a 'weathered' look no-one will notice its flaws anyway! Other 'antique' items can also be called into service as plant pots once you have added the essential drainage holes, i.e. tin baths, galvanised buckets, watering cans, colanders (they have ready made holes and make great hanging baskets).

Wooden containers and troughs are natural looking and look attractive in most situations. Window boxes also fall into this category. Purpose made ones should ideally have been pressure treated to ensure a longer life because the timber will be exposed to both the weather and the water used on the vegetables. The exceptions to this are hardwoods such as oak and chestnut which are much more resistant. It is a good idea to line wooden containers with a sheet of polythene (with a few holes punched in it) before you fill them with soil. This will provide the wood with added protection from the damp soil and will make it easier for you to lift out the old compost at the end of the growing season once your vegetables have been harvested.

Plastic containers and pots are ideal for roof gardens and balconies as they are much lighter than most other materials. The main drawbacks are that this also makes them more likely to blow over in windy conditions and they can also become brittle after 2 or 3 years use. However, they are a lot cheaper to buy in the first place and can be easily replaced. Perhaps not a choice if you want your containers to be as ecologically sound as your vegetable growing.

Use your imagination. All manner of items can be used or turned into perfect growing places for organic vegetables – I have already mentioned old watering cans and Wellington boots. Tall plastic buckets cut down to a required size or used as they are, are ideal for growing potatoes on the patio.

For a modern look, metallic containers in different shapes and sizes and brimming over with leafy vegetables can give a bold and very striking effect.

If you want your brand new terracotta pots to have a natural, 'lived in' look, try painting on some diluted liquid manure (see the section on liquid feeds p.137) or natural yoghurt which will provide the perfect environment for lichens and mosses to grow.

Grow bags have been around for years and are easy and inexpensive places for growing your vegetables. Of course they aren't great to look at, but they can easily be disguised in amongst other pots and containers. When choosing your grow bags, choose the biggest size you can and don't go for the budget ones. The larger volume of compost in a more expensive one will mean the plants you put in them won't dry out so quickly and it is definitely better to pay a little more for better quality compost. Don't restrict yourself to growing only the traditional vegetables like tomatoes and cucumbers in them either – they make ideal containers for things like runner or French climbing beans because the bags can be positioned to fit snugly against a fence or a wall and the plants trained up as they grow.

Size of containers

Generally, the deeper your container or pot, the wider the range of vegetables you will be able to grow in it. Vegetables with small root systems such as lettuce can be grown in shallower vessels, but this makes them more prone to drying out which can spell disaster as lettuce hold very little moisture reserves in their leaves. This also means that you will have to be watering more often. The minimum depth for any vegetable pot is probably no less than 30cm (12 inches), and much more than that for deeper rooting varieties (see Chapter 4).

The total surface area of the container is important too; all vegetables must be spaced according to their requirements – many can be grown in smaller spaces but will then need to be harvested before they are fully mature. Varieties of 'baby veg' can be specially developed to produce smaller cropping varieties or others that can be picked when immature, so taking up much less growing space. If you are thinking about growing your own crop of potatoes, another option is to buy a ready made kit. It is possible to purchase a growing bag, compost and seed potatoes all ready for planting yourself. The woven green polybag can be sited anywhere and makes 'digging' your potatoes easy.

Essential care

Looking after your containers during the growing season and afterwards is really important, because not only will it prolong their life, but keeping them clean and hygienic will ensure that the crops you grow in them are less likely to suffer from pests and diseases.

Once you have emptied out the old compost from the pot, they will need to be thoroughly scrubbed out with a brush using a biodegradable detergent. Once you have rinsed them, leave to dry naturally. To get rid of any final 'nasties' I use a natural cleaner specifically to kill any disease spores. A good one is called Citrox, which can also be used to disinfect greenhouses, tools, seed trays and it won't harm your plants! Once again leave the pots to dry. Then they can be stored somewhere out of the elements; if this is not possible then stand them upside down which will protect them from damage in severe frosts. When re-using them again in the spring, check your pots for slugs and snails which may have been hibernating inside. These pests are very fond of succulent

Flowerpot Farming

young plants and can destroy lots in a single night. Do yourself a favour and don't let them get the chance to eat yours!

Seeds

Perhaps this should have been first in this list because of course seeds really are THE most important item. You can buy packets of seed from many outlets these days; garden centres, supermarkets, or mail order from the seed merchants themselves. As well as this you can also get hold of unusual and heirloom varieties not generally available to the public via retail by becoming a member of a seed library or seed swap group. You can also raise your own plants by saving seed from some of last year's crop which you have allowed to run to seed for precisely this purpose (although not from modern F1 varieties – I'll explain more about this in chapter 4).

For your first attempts at vegetable growing, I'd recommend buying packets of seed from the sources mentioned above. That way you'll know that the seed they contain is fresh. It's also a good idea to request catalogues from at least two seed suppliers (addresses at the back) then you can browse at leisure and compare varieties side by side before you make your final choices. Yes, I know you can browse their on-line catalogues, but for me nothing can beat sitting back with a real catalogue – it's more relaxing for one thing and I don't have to worry about spilling my tea on my computer keyboard!

Once I've made my choice, I'll then usually order on-line, though.

These packets will carry clear and concise growing instructions, not to mention a pretty colour picture on the front of the vegetable you will hopefully eventually be eating and it is reassuring to see what you are aiming for. Most new packets of seed contain an inner foil pack holding the seed itself. Inside, the seed stays viable for much longer until the pack is opened and normal ageing starts. Don't panic though, because many vegetable seeds can be kept for a year or even more until they deteriorate too much to germinate successfully.

You can also collect your seeds direct from the plant. Tomatoes, cucumbers and most other fruits and vegetables, as well as flowers, self-seed. So why not harvest them yourself? Just collect them in a brown paper bag, seal, label and date them and then store them in a dark, dry cupboard until it's time for planting. If using this method it is wise to also introduce some fresh seeds from time to time.

Check the back of the seed packet

How many seeds does it contain? When do you need to sow (i.e. is it already too late to sow them this year)? How much heat do the seeds need to germinate (you can keep the seed trays indoors until they do)? When can they be planted outside and where? Does it give details of the ultimate height and spread of the plant, very important information if you are growing in containers. Are the other cultural instructions clear (not so important once you have grown them before, but reassuring to have when starting out)? Harvesting time? Some even have a little description of the vegetables, from the succinct: Unwins autumn cabbage 'Winnigstadt' – "robust flavour, solid, pointed heads", to the more descriptive: Mr Fothergill's climbing bean 'Blue Lake' - "an excellent white seeded variety, well known for its flavour, it produces heavy crops of round, stringless pods. Left to mature the dried beans can be used as haricots. Ideal for deep freezing".

Storing seed

Even unopened seed packets should be kept in as cool and dry conditions as possible. Damp sheds and overly hot rooms with fluctuating temperatures should be avoided. An ideal place is a cool spare room. The packets are best stored in airtight tins or jars. Loose, saved seed should be collected in small paper bags or envelopes (never in plastic) and again stored in an airtight container. A refrigerator is another good place to store seed, but bear in mind that if you are saving it from one year to another it will be there a long time, perhaps taking up valuable space. Some varieties of vegetable can be stored longer than others, even in ideal conditions – see Appendix for a list of seed life expectancy by vegetable.

Chapter Four
From Seed to Harvest

Seeds are wonderful things and the magic of raising a whole lot of vegetables from just a handful of seed is one of nature's greatest feats and something that never fails to amaze me each year. There is no mystique about growing vegetables from seed, you just need to follow a few basic common-sense rules and techniques and success will be yours. It's true that some vegetables are easier to grow than others – but there is really no reason why you won't be able to successfully get good crops from any of the plants listed in this chapter, whether you are growing in containers or not.

Most types of vegetable now have at least one or two varieties that have been developed in dwarf or compact versions. Something else to look out for when you are choosing seed is the Royal Horticultural Society's 'Award of Garden Merit', indicated by a symbol on selected varieties of vegetable seed. This award is given to plants deemed to be of outstanding excellence for use in ordinary gardens. The plants are rated for hardiness, resistance to pests and diseases, good availability and all-round value for the home gardener. These tried and tested varieties are a good starting point for your first steps into raising vegetables, but don't be put off from experimenting with <u>any</u> type of vegetable that takes your fancy.

Most of your vegetables can be raised from seed indoors in seed trays placed on a bright, warm windowsill. These conditions will heat up the compost, ensuring good germination. Even if you are planning to grow most of your vegetables in an outside bed, you can use the same method and transplant the young vegetables once they are large enough and have been acclimatised to the outside conditions. Later on, perhaps you might like to invest in a small propagator, a heated box especially made for raising plants from seed. These can be set to varying temperatures according to different plant requirements and are very useful if you want to bring plants on a little earlier than usual. However, for your first steps into flowerpot farming, covered trays or pots on a windowsill will do very nicely.

Some vegetables can be sown directly into their final containers instead of first being started off indoors, and this will save you both time and compost. However, you will need to make sure that all risk of frost is past and that the vegetables are hardy enough to be grown this way. All varieties suited to direct sowing outside in the ground are OK for direct container sowing. Not recommended for this method because they need higher temperatures to germinate successfully are tomatoes, cucumbers, aubergines and peppers.

Sowing seeds in spring

Spring is the busiest time of the gardening year and a critical one at that. If seeds are sown too early outside and late frosts occur, then some less hardy vegetables could be severely set back or even killed. Sowing too early indoors might not seem such a risk, but having to hold back seedlings inside for a couple of weeks longer because the weather has not warmed up sufficiently for them to be planted out, might mean that they grow too fast and become stretched and weakened – never recovering sufficiently to produce decent crops when the time comes.

Sowing indoors no more than a month or so before the last frosts are expected should ensure that your seedlings will be at a perfect stage to plant out when the weather is right. Getting the timing right is something of a gamble for gardeners both old and new because no two years are ever the same. Following the advice given on the seed packets and following the weather forecasts is the best we growers can do!

Tips and techniques for growing indoors

As well as purpose made seed trays, you can sow your seed in ordinary flowerpots too – in fact, vegetables with medium to large sized seed are better suited to this as their root systems are larger and need a lot more room. Sowing two seeds to a pot is recommended for large seeds; if both germinate they can always be carefully separated at the time of planting into their final containers or outside.

1.   Fill your trays with a good quality seed compost or multi-purpose compost and firm it down lightly.

Flowerpot Farming

2.   Follow the guidance given on the seed packets for the best months to sow and for spacing the seed and depth to sow.

3.   As a general rule, large seeds are buried (the bigger they are the deeper they go) whilst small seed can be sown on top of the compost with the merest amount of sieved compost over it.

4.   Water the trays or pots gently using a can with a fine rose – the compost should be moist, not wet, and the seeds need to stay where you sowed them!

5.   You can now choose to cover your trays or pots by either covering with a sheet of glass or by placing a clear polythene bag over each pot, secured with a rubber band. Both ways help to keep moisture in and raise the temperature inside the glass or polythene bag high enough to encourage germination. Don't forget to label the trays so you know which vegetable is in each one, how many seeds you have sown and the date you sowed them.

6.   Place the containers on a windowsill where they can stay undisturbed until the first shoots start emerging through the soil surface. As soon as this happens remove the bag or the glass cover, but make sure the plants are protected from strong sunlight. As they grow you will need to turn them regularly, making sure the plants receive the same amount of light on all sides and grow uniformly. If they are left in one position they will 'stretch' towards the light and the plants closest to the window will grow tall and leggy while the ones furthest away will grow very slowly in comparison.

7.   If you are growing your young plants in seed trays, once they reach the 'four leaf' stage, i.e. two initial seed leaves plus a set of 'true' leaves, it will be time to 'prick them out'. All this means is that you re-plant them carefully into a larger pot or container to allow them to grow on a bit. Use a dibber to gently lever the seedlings out. Always hold the plants by their leaves rather than

the stem which is very delicate, particularly at this early stage. It is better to damage one leaf than the main stem and ruin the whole plant.

Any larger seeds in individual pots can be left to grow on until either a) they become too big for the pots and need to be repotted into larger ones, or b) they can be planted into their final positions after hardening off. The same goes for seeds sown in module trays which should have enough room to expand as long as a single plant is in each module.

Hardening off

Once the weather is warmer (depending on how far North you live) you can put the young plants outside during the daytime, remembering to bring them in again at night. This will acclimatise them to the outside conditions and a couple of weeks should be enough, after which they can stay outside permanently and be potted on into their final positions in the garden or in containers. A cold frame, if you are lucky enough to have one or have room enough for one, is an ideal solution for hardening off your plants without the need for bringing them in and out morning and night. The cold frame lid can be kept closed when the plants are placed inside it initially, gradually increasing the ventilation by opening the lid over the next couple of weeks. Proceed as for the previous method.

Remember that all vegetables started off indoors will need to be hardened off for a couple of weeks before planting them in their final positions.

Preparing your containers for vegetable crops

Always make sure your containers are thoroughly cleaned before you re-use them as this will ensure that there are

Flowerpot Farming

no nasty pests and diseases lurking in them, ready to prey on your vegetables. Scrub them out thoroughly and make sure there are adequate drainage holes in the bottom and that if there are, they are not blocked up.

If the container is a large one, place a layer of broken clay pots at the bottom if you have any to hand, or large pebbles or stones to create a good drainage system. If you are using smaller pots, a layer of large gravel or stones should be adequate. Then fill up the container to about 2.5cm (1") from the top with good quality multi-purpose compost, and a little organic compost or a small amount of rotted manure if you have any to mix in with it.

Now we get to the exciting part – planting the vegetables in their final positions! Water the seed or module trays, pots, etc. containing the young plants an hour or so before you want to re-pot them. This will make them easier to remove without using undue pressure to get them out. Small plants in pots are easily removed by tipping them upside down while supporting the plant and soil as the pot is removed. Plants growing in modules can be teased out by gently but firmly pinching the section of the module underneath the plant. This should free them up and they can then be easily removed.

Make holes in the compost in the new container at the correct spacing and place the plants into them. Make sure that the roots are at the correct depth with the top of the root ball just under the surface of the soil. Next firm down the compost, adding a little more on top if required. Finally, water the compost thoroughly – and the job is done!

Preparing your garden soil for sowing outside.

We have already discussed ways to improve your soil earlier in this book, so I hope that once the time is right for your vegetables to be planted outside into the big wide world, the soil they are destined to be planted in is already in the best possible condition. The following instructions can also be applied to raised beds.

Choose a fine, dry day for sowing when the soil has warmed up sufficiently in spring to encourage germination. If there are already weed seeds coming up, then the soil is definitely warm enough, and you will have to pull or hoe them out! Rake over the soil to break down any big clods of earth – you are aiming for a fine 'tilth' which is gardener-speak for a fine, crumbly texture.

Using a garden line to mark a straight line across the bed, use the corner of a rake or hoe to make a shallow drill alongside the string. The depth of drill will depend on the variety of seed you are sowing. Open the seed packet and pour the seeds into your palm, placing them at the suggested sowing distance for that particular vegetable. Larger seeds are much less fiddly to sow than tiny ones, but try to get them spaced out as evenly as possible (although you will be able to thin them out once they grow). Once your row is completely sown, cover the seeds with the soil using the back of the rake or hoe.

Don't forget to mark the row with a plant label so you know exactly where and what they are.

Once the seeds have germinated and the vegetables are large enough to handle, you can remove any excess plants to give the remaining ones plenty of room to grow and mature. If you are careful, you can replant these somewhere else if you have the space. In the case of lettuce, spinach, beetroot and similar vegetables, the tasty young leaves from any thinnings need not be wasted and can be added to salads or stir fries. Try to weed around your vegetable rows regularly, because if they are left to grow, weeds will compete for nutrients and water and can also harbour pests such as slugs and snails.

Transplanting your vegetables outside.

Much of the above also applies to transplanting young vegetable plants outside. Ideally the soil should be slightly moist, not wet (you can do a lot of damage to the soil structure by walking over it when wet) when you plant, but the vegetables should be watered in once they are in place so they are not struggling for moisture straight away.

Again, aim for a smooth soil surface with a reasonably fine tilth – not quite so important as for seed beds but large clods are definitely not desirable and are extremely hard to break up in the summer months if left to dry out. If planting in straight rows then a garden line will be an essential piece of equipment. The final planting distances should be as given on the seed packet.

Growing vegetables for the very first time is rather exciting and most definitely rewarding, but also slightly concerning if you are not sure exactly when you should be doing what. After your first year, particularly if you keep a notebook as I suggested in Chapter 3, you will have a pretty good idea when is exactly the right time to carry out your sowing and planting jobs and, best of all, it will be unique to your own situation and climate.

Great vegetables and fruit for small spaces

The following is a list of fruit and vegetables that can be grown in limited spaces as well as outside. When you are choosing your seeds, look out in particular for varieties especially bred for good use of space. For example, crops that can be picked as 'baby veg', either ready for harvest before reaching maturity or dwarf and low-growing varieties. There are new introductions each year and these will be highlighted in the seed catalogues, so do look out for them.

Fruit trees

Fruit trees on your patio, balcony or in the garden bring the added bonus of attractive blossom when they flower in the spring as well as a supply of fruit to harvest in the autumn or winter. By choosing varieties grafted onto dwarfing rootstocks, most popular fruit will grow well in a large container or pot. Most fruit trees are grafted onto rootstocks – this determines the eventual size of the tree and also maximises its cropping potential. Fruit trees in their natural state will not produce anything like the amount of fruit as one grafted onto a rootstock will. More detail on rootstocks for particular types of fruit is provided later in this chapter. Annual pruning to keep the trees in shape and topdressing (mulching) each winter with a 5-10cm (2-4") layer of organic compost or well rotted manure (do not let this actually touch the base of the tree) will be all the maintenance it needs to keep it healthy.

Most fruit trees offered for sale will be two years or older and will be either pot grown or supplied bare rooted. Specialist fruit tree nurseries generally have the best choice of varieties and rootstocks, and if you buy from them via mail order the trees you receive will almost certainly be bare rooted. Bare rooted trees need to be planted between November and early March when they are dormant and will need to have their roots soaked in a bucket of water for an hour or so before planting.

Planting a fruit tree direct into your garden

You will need to dig a hole approximately two spades deep and 50cm (20") in diameter. Loosen up the soil at the bottom and sides of the hole and fork in a handful of bonemeal. Even dwarfing rootstocks need staking, so drive in a 5cm (2") diameter post into the hole before you plant the tree. This way you won't damage the roots.

Position the tree in the hole, making sure that the point where the tree is grafted onto its rootstock is not buried; you should be able to see a clear indication of the level up to which the soil previously came on the trunk. Fill in the hole with soil and firm it in with your foot. Using a rubber tie, attach the tree to the stake. Water the tree well and make sure it remains well watered, particularly during its first few summers. The rubber tie will also need adjusting on occasion as the tree grows.

Container grown fruit trees

Containers should be as big as possible with a minimum depth of 45-60cm (18-24"); half a wooden barrel is ideal. Fill the bottom with clay crocks or large stones to help drainage. You can use good quality topsoil mixed with a handful of bonemeal and well-rotted manure. The soil itself should be free draining, and the tree should be mulched with more organic matter each year. Keep the soil moist, especially in hot, dry weather and when the fruits are forming. Pruning should be carried out over the winter months, aiming to cut out any branches that are crossing or growing into the tree and causing congestion. Pruning will keep the tree to a compact size and will also help cut down wind resistance - if your plant is in a pot the likelihood of it being blown over will therefore be reduced. You should be looking to end up with a nice, open symmetrical goblet shape. A point to note is that some apples fruit on the tips of their branches while other varieties do so on 'spurs' which appear along the length of the branches at intervals. Check which category your tree falls into and prune accordingly, i.e. if tip bearing, ensure some of the tips are left for fruit to form the following year.

Apples

Dwarfing rootstocks make it possible to grow apple varieties grafted onto them in containers and cramped situations. M27 and M9 are the ones to choose for this purpose. 'Family' apple trees can have several different varieties of apple grafted onto one rootstock. If you want to plant straight out in the garden and would like a bigger tree, then one of the more vigorous rootstocks is M26 which will grow to 10-12ft or MM106, a semi-vigorous one for average sized gardens which will reach 14-18 ft in height.

If you only have room for one tree, then make sure it is self-fertile or you will need a pollination partner (another apple tree flowering at the same time) to cross pollinate it. If your neighbours have apple trees in their gardens then pollination may not be a problem. You can buy your trees in pots from a nursery or garden centre, although they may stock only the more popular varieties. Specialist tree nurseries generally supply bare rooted specimens only by mail order, but have a wider choice. Bare rooted trees need to be planted when dormant, i.e. between November and February, but pot grown ones can be re-potted or planted at any time of the year.

As far as varieties go you will need to decide whether you want early, mid or late cropping apples and dessert or cooking apples. Generally the earlier the crop, the shorter the storage life of the fruit. Late season apples can keep well into the following year if stored in good conditions.

Here is a selection of varieties available, although the specialist fruit nurseries stock many more. Perhaps there is a particular apple you have always liked the sound of and want to grow.

Dessert (eating) apples:
Ashmead's Kernel: a sweet, aromatic flavour, yellow flesh, firm and crisp, skin green/yellow flushed with orange. Crops December-March.
Egremont Russet: a golden russet fruit of medium size with a delicious and distinctive flavour. Crops well from

October-December.
Beauty of Bath: sweet, juicy and pleasantly sharp with a pale yellow skin, flushed with bright red. Heavy crops are ready in early August.

Culinary (cooking) apples:
Bramley's seedling: this one hardly needs an introduction with big crops, firm yellow flesh and a wonderful flavour. The fruit is ready from November.
Howgate Wonder: a large yellow/green fruit flushed with red and first class for cooking.
Dual purpose (suitable for cooking & eating):
James Grieve: if picked early this makes a good cooking apple and for dessert use it is tender, juicy and with an excellent flavour. Ready in September.

Other fruit trees and bushes

The planting advice above can also be followed when establishing other tree and bush fruit.

Pears

The ideal pears for container growing are those varieties grafted onto the rootstock Quince C. The more vigorous Quince A is much better suited to direct planting. Pears in containers will need to be placed in a slightly more sheltered position than apples but in other aspects the two fruits are very similar. In general, pears need less pruning than apples – perhaps more of a 'tidy up' than a serious pruning session just to keep them in shape. Like apples, pears normally need a pollination partner to produce fruit. The varieties 'Conference' and 'Concorde' are most often offered for sale, but there are others; try 'Beth' – an ideal garden pear, or 'Invincible' which is extremely hardy and self-fertile.

Flowerpot Farming

Apricots, Peaches and Nectarines

The fruit trees in this group may sound exotic and therefore difficult to grow in cooler climates, but they are all capable of producing a decent crop in the UK. Peaches are the hardiest of the lot and can be grown out on an open site. The only problem comes with early flowering varieties that are susceptible to late frosts. The way to guarantee getting a crop with these is to protect the flowers during the cold nights by covering them with horticultural fleece, but it is far easier to select a late flowering variety in the first place. 'Peregrine' is one of the best choices for growing in the UK and usually flowers after the last frosts. The pink blossoms provide an eye-catching display in the spring and beautiful red flushed yellow/white skinned fruits in August. It is also a good choice for training against a wall.

Apricots and nectarines are more tender trees and better situated in a south-facing border or courtyard. If trained against a wall then so much the better, to make the most of any heat retained within it. Cultivars developed for growing in cooler climates are worth searching for. A good choice of apricot is 'Flavourcot', late flowering and producing huge crops of delicious orange/red fruits in August. It is excellent both for eating fresh and cooking. 'Fantasia' is one of the best nectarines for garden settings, is very easy to grow and has a degree of resistance to frost. Its orange/red fruits with juicy yellow flesh and a 'free' stone are ready for picking in August.

Peaches, apricots and nectarines are all good subjects for containers, and have the added advantage that they can be moved under protection if frosts threaten. Their soil requirements are the same as for other fruit trees in large pots and containers and they can be pruned heavily during the winter to keep a compact size, so long as they are well fed and watered. Mulch the surface of the containers each winter with a top dressing of compost or well-rotted manure to replenish the nutrients the tree will need the following season.

Cherries

A dwarfing rootstock such as 'Giesla 5' makes it possible to grow cherries in a pot on the patio and of course outside in the garden. Self-fertile dessert varieties are a good choice such as 'Stella' or 'Sunburst', but they do need to be sited in a sunny spot in order for the fruit to ripen. Not so the culinary variety 'Morello' which can be fan trained against a north facing wall as long as they are not subjected to frost. A well drained soil is required, and cherries will need plenty of water in the summer.

Citrus Fruit (Oranges, Mandarins, Lemons)

Mini citrus trees are ideal for container growing as long as you have the space to bring them indoors somewhere warm and well lit during the winter months. They aren't suitable for growing permanently outside because they are so tender, but full size specimens are successful when grown in glasshouses.

Buy pot grown specimens from garden centres and specialist nurseries and plant them in terracotta pots as they prefer a well aerated soil that is rich and drains easily. Small citrus trees are very attractive, with wonderful scented leaves, flowers and fruit and so are wonderful additions to sunny windowsills, patios and balconies in the summer. Move them outside in spring and back indoors in October before the first frosts.

Flowerpot Farming

Keep the trees well trimmed, cutting back hard before spring growth starts. Straggly branches can break under the weight of fruit if not trimmed back. Feed regularly with a seaweed liquid feed through summer and autumn.

Figs

For a touch of the Mediterranean, look no further than a fig tree. They do best in a sunny position and kept sheltered from heavy frosts during the winter. Unlike many of the fruit trees, figs are not grafted onto rootstocks but can be confined to a pot which will restrict their growth, but increase the chance of bigger crops (all the vigour will be channelled into producing fruit rather than growing the tree itself). The pot needs to be a sturdy one because the confined roots could possibly break through some of the thinner materials.

They also make a dramatic feature when fan trained against a wall. Large fruit crops will ripen in July and August; in the UK climate these will have formed on the tree the previous year, ripening the next and producing sweet and juicy figs with a deep red flesh under their brown skins. Two popular varieties are 'Brown Turkey' which is very hardy, and a compact fig called 'Prolific' which is recommended especially for growing in tubs and pots.

Soft Fruit

Soft fruit is very rewarding to grow yourself. Things like gooseberries, blueberries, and red/white/blackcurrants are rarely seen in the shops and when they are they command a very high price and are more often than not imported from overseas. So what if you only have room enough for one plant – choose the one you like best to eat and it will provide a delicious, in-season crop that you certainly wouldn't otherwise have had. And the fruit will be the freshest you have ever tasted, especially if you pick and eat it straight from the plant. A word of warning, however; you will not be the only one to appreciate the ripening fruits when the time comes – BE PREPARED TO PROTECT YOUR CROP BY COVERING THEM WITH NETTING OR THE BIRDS WILL GET TO THEM FIRST!

All the soft fruit listed below will thrive in outdoor beds where plenty of organic matter has been dug in. Many of them are suitable for container growing as long as a soil depth of at least 12" (30cm) can be provided. All fruit bushes, wherever they are planted, will benefit from a top dressing of well rotted manure/garden compost each winter to maintain fertility.

Soft fruit for growing in containers

Strawberries

You don't need stacks of room for growing strawberries; they can be as at home in a small container on the patio as they are in the vegetable plot – and because they are low-growing plants you can even put them in hanging baskets and grow bags. Perhaps the most attractive container to grow them in is a traditional strawberry pot, a curved terracotta urn with lipped holes arranged at intervals around the outside. Using pots and containers has the added benefit of keeping the plants off the ground and out of reach of slugs and the fruits are also less likely to be affected by mildew caused by damp conditions. Plants grown at ground level are traditionally mulched with barley straw when the fruits are developing to keep them off the soil and away from mildew and slugs – you will have seen this done if you have ever been to a 'pick-

Flowerpot Farming

your-own' strawberry farm.

You can buy your plants for your own garden in pots from nurseries and garden centres and these can be planted at any time of the year. Just keep them watered regularly to help them establish and during dry spells in the summer. There are two main types of strawberry; summer fruiting and perpetual cropping (or everbearing). The summer fruiters usually produce one large crop ('flush') of fruit any time between late May and late July depending on the variety. Perpetuals bear one crop in June then another in late summer or early autumn.

Strawberries remain productive for around 3 years or so and are then best replaced with new plants. You can propagate new plants yourself from 'runners' which are baby plants produced each year by the original plant. If they are growing in open soil then they should root by themselves at the point they touch the soil, but if the strawberries are in containers you can assist them to root by placing a flower pot full of moist potting compost close to the container and gently fixing the young plant against the soil with a small piece of wire to hold it in place. In about 4 weeks roots should have formed and you will have a brand new strawberry plant.

Site your strawberries in a sunny, sheltered site in rich soil or compost that is free draining as they really hate cold and damp conditions.

Selected varieties:
Summer fruiting: 'Elsanta', 'Honeoye' (both early), 'Cambridge Favourite' (main season).
Perpetual; 'Aromel', 'Calypso'.

Raspberries

There's nothing like freshly picked raspberries straight from your garden and served with cream on a pleasant summer's afternoon! Raspberries crop for between 3 and 6 weeks in the fruiting season, and each cane (plant) can remain productive for up to 12 years so they could serve you well if you are willing to spend a little time on pruning after they have finished fruiting and keeping the soil fertility high around them by adding yearly doses of organic matter. Choosing your varieties carefully could also mean raspberries from early July to the first frosts.

There are two distinct types; summer or autumn fruiting - if you have some open space in your garden then you will be able to grow them both if you want to. Container growing is best suited to the autumn varieties. Autumn cropping raspberry canes are cut down to the ground once fruiting has finished, unlike the summer ones on which only the old canes which have fruited are removed. The new canes have to be left unpruned until the following year because it is on these that the new fruit will form. The bare canes can look a little unsightly in a pot, but if you aren't too worried about that and can provide the canes with some support throughout the year, then go for the summer ones too.

Raspberries grow best in full sun, but will grow in partial shade if they have to. Soil rich in organic matter is ideal and if you are growing in containers, then the deeper the better – at least 30 cm (12") minimum. They are mainly offered for sale as bare rooted canes which need to be planted as soon as possible, ideally between November and December or, failing that, in March. Sometimes you will see container grown specimens and these can be planted at any time. Make sure the canes are planted

Flowerpot Farming

at the correct level – look out for the old soil mark, and firm them in.

Varieties to look out for are reliable names such as 'Glen Ample', a mid season and relatively spineless raspberry, 'Malling Jewel', another mid-season variety with fairly compact growth and reliable and traditional and 'Malling Leo', a later summer fruiting crop (late July-early August) with an exceptional taste and resistant to aphids and viral diseases. Highly recommended for fruit from August to the first frosts is 'Autumn Bliss' with excellent tasting and firm fruits that keep well after picking. For novelty value 'Fallgold' is a yellow autumn fruiting raspberry.

Blueberries

The blueberry is becoming more fashionable now but is still a fairly unusual soft fruit to grow at home. High in vitamin C, blueberries are great eaten fresh and can be used for making jam. The plants carry attractive spring blossom, striking fruit and a blazing red leaf colour in autumn.

Blueberries can be very worthwhile in containers because they need a distinctly acid soil and these conditions can be created more easily in a confined space. Ericaceous compost can be bought in garden centres (normally used for acid loving plants such as Rhododendrons and Azaleas). Once the blueberry is planted the soil needs to be kept moist by using soft water or rain water only (if you live in a hard water area, don't use tap water).

There are several different varieties, with cropping periods spanning from July through to September. The average height of a blueberry bush is 1 metre, but there are compact varieties such as 'Top Hat' which only reaches 50cm and is ideal for the patio.

Gooseberries

Over time gooseberries grow into quite substantial bushes which is fine if you have the room to plant them in a dedicated soft fruit bed or a large border. As with most fruit trees and bushes, they lose their leaves in late autumn, so are not the most attractive things to look at through the winter and early spring. An alternative to a bush is to train them to grow as a cordon with 1-3 upright stems or into a fan shape again a wall or support which will make them more suited to small space or container growing. Gooseberries have notoriously prickly stems though, and you will need to be armed with a stout pair of garden gloves before you tackle any pruning.

A site where the gooseberries will receive full sun is ideal, but partial shade is tolerated. One bush will yield between 6-12 lb and a cordon around 3lb of fruit and should remain productive for at least 10 years.

Most garden centres stock the popular varieties of gooseberry and you can choose from dessert and culinary ones and also either green or red/black fruit (which are normally sweeter).

Grapes

It is certainly possible to grow a grapevine in a container and get several bunches of grapes from it every season. I once had a grapevine that was trained up and around a doorway leading into a small conservatory. The vine was planted in a large plastic barrel which was either brought into a small unheated greenhouse during the winter or the pot wrapped up in bubble wrap (this happened more often once the vine was so long and unwieldy that it got too tricky for two of us to transport across the garden!).

Grapevines can become too rampant and vigorous if they are grown outside in very rich soil – but restricting their roots in a container makes them more controllable. After several years, and a house move, my grapevine (variety 'Black Hamburg') is still going strong today, but is now planted outside and trained up a south facing pergola in the garden.

You could certainly do the same with a grapevine on a balcony or a patio, provided there is lots of late summer and autumn sun to help the grapes to ripen. The lush, lime green leaves are very attractive in the summer and look wonderful trained against a wall, bringing a touch of the exotic to anywhere they are planted with the bunches of grapes being almost a bonus.

Seasonal care

Apart from careful watering through the year (if container grown), by far the most important task you must do is to keep your vine pruned. There is quite an art to pruning grapevines and there are many variations, but there is no need to get bogged down with all that unless you become a grapevine enthusiast! Vines are surprisingly tough once they get established and inaccurate pruning certainly won't kill it. The simplest way to grow your vine is as a cordon; a central stem 'leader' trained upwards to form the support for the vine. In the first two years after planting the tips of each of the laterals (side shoots) are cut back, leaving five leaves in spring and any flowers removed, then between November and December the laterals should be cut right back to about 2.5cm (1") from the leader. The new growth on the leader should be cut by a half. In the years following that, the basic routine is applied and by then each lateral will have at least one flowering spur. If there are more just rub them off.

Treating your vine with an organic liquid feed from the time the fruit starts to form until it ripens will be very beneficial. Be sure to cover the fruit with netting to protect it from the birds.

Good outdoor varieties that do well in the UK as well as the 'Black Hamburg' (a dessert variety with large, juicy black grapes) are 'Boskoop Glory' (a consistently good cropper with black dessert grapes) and 'Seyval' (a green grape suited to winemaking and eating fresh which makes a light and fruity wine and is a reliable grapevine for colder areas). Vines can be bought from mail order nurseries specialising in fruit (who will offer a wider choice of varieties) or from a garden centre as a potted specimen.

Currants: Black, Red and White

Blackcurrants are still a rarity in the shops and you will probably only ever get to taste red and white currants if you grow your own. You will, however, be able to make some delicious desserts, pies, jams, jellies, and wines with the fruit.

All varieties of currants can be grown in large pots and containers but they will need to measure at least 30cm (1ft) in depth to get a successful crop. Although we might think of them as closely related and therefore similar in their cultivation needs, this is not quite true. Whereas white and red currants are very forgiving plants, able to survive in relatively poor soil (but a bit of organic matter incorporated into the soil or container compost will definitely be appreciated), blackcurrants need a very rich and free draining one and mulching around the plants each winter is a must.

Keep all currant bushes pruned to shape, particularly if you are growing them in containers because they can become very large indeed. However, once again you need to prune differently. White and redcurrants will fruit on new growth so, no matter how badly you prune them, you should get some sort of crop! Blackcurrants are more fussy and fruit on one year old growth so you will have to make sure that some old wood is left. All pruning is done in the dormant season between November and March.

Netting your crops will be an absolute necessity if you want to eat any yourself.

Varieties:
Blackcurrants: 'Laxton's Giant' produces large berries, 'Ben Sarek' (mid-season), 'Ben Lomond' (late) and 'Ben More' (very late) are relatively new varieties with better disease resistance and more productive.

Whitecurrants: 'White Versailles' is a reliable, pale, sweet fruit, ideal in fruit salads and ready in early July.

Redcurrants: 'Redstart' has bright red fruits, consistent yields and cropsin mid-August.

Blackberries

These are rather tricky to grow in containers as they are vigorous, scrambling plants. They could be planted in a pot and tied in securely against a wall or trellis, but being confined in this way is not an ideal situation for them. By far the best thing is to plant them direct into a rich, free-draining soil which has had lots of manure dug into it. They are very hardy plants with very few problems. Birds will eat them but the berries are produced in such large quantities that there is usually plenty for all, which makes it ideal for the gardener who wants to attract wildlife as well as produce some food for himself. Pruning is simple: the fruit is formed on both new and old wood so cut out all the old and dead stuff over the winter and train the new growth where you want it.

The majority of blackberry varieties are very prickly and harvesting and cutting back is not such an easy task, although there are thornless types such as 'Oregon Thornless'. 'Bedford Giant' is an early variety (ripening in late summer) and 'John Innes' is less vigorous and crops later.

Vegetables

I will start our list with the summer cropping vegetables, which I guess are the most popular choices for most people starting out on a vegetable growing adventure. They make the most of our relatively short summer and produce the sort of vegetables perfect for eating at this time of the year. Welcome to the salad vegetables...

Salad Leaves

Very successful when grown in containers, salad leaves and lettuces are great in window boxes and small spaces in borders as well as in vegetable beds both raised or traditional. There are different types of lettuce; the butterhead (smooth, soft leaves and rounded, compact hearts), Batavia (open outer growth but crisp heart), cos (crisp, longer, narrower leaves), crisphead (an iceberg type with dense, solid heart) and loose leaf (fast growing,

Flowerpot Farming

non-hearting, cut-and-come again leaves to harvest over several weeks).

Indoors, seed can be sown early in the year from early March onwards right through until the autumn. They dislike being transplanted so are better sown singly in module trays, one seed per module – that way root disturbance is kept to a minimum when the young plants are relocated to their final growing positions.

For summer and autumn lettuces you can sow outside from late March to late July. If you plan to raise them from seed indoors for transplanting into containers/window boxes/pots at a later stage then you can sow as early as late February – this will give you an earlier crop from mid-May onwards. Lettuce seed is fairly small and needs to be sown into shallow drills in finely prepared soil. It is difficult to sow them thinly as the seed is quite light and not that easy to handle, but it will save you too much thinning out of the plants once they have reached the true leaf stage. The plants can be grown in containers as little as 10cm (4") deep. Always harden off any lettuce raised indoors before transplanting outside.

There are also winter hardy types which you can carry on harvesting throughout the winter: 'Winter Density', 'Winter Crop' and 'Rouge d'Hiver' are all winter hardy lettuces, so it is possible to have fresh lettuces from your garden all year round. In particularly exposed spots in hard winters I would recommend covering the plants with horticultural fleece or a cloche if at all possible to give them some added protection.

If you would like a small selection of different lettuces rather than buying whole seed packets of each variety, look out for the mixed packs that are available; they will have the added advantage of maturing at slightly different times, avoiding a glut which would occur if they were all ready for eating at the same time.

Should you decide to stick to one or two favourite varieties it is a good idea to sow your seeds in small batches every 2-4 weeks instead of all at once – if you get into a glut situation some lettuce is bound to get wasted, but a steady supply will be manageable and more welcome.

Cut and come again types such as the salad bowl lettuce can be harvested as baby leaves which will encourage the production of more leaves over several weeks and others like the iceberg and cos are picked whole.

The array of colours ranging from pale to dark green through to leaves tinged with pink and deep maroon hues means that the plants are decorative as well as edible, particularly in the flower border or window box. Dwarf varieties such as the butterhead type 'Tom Thumb' (dating back to 1885) or cos 'Little Gem' are ideal for growing in small spaces and they are both quick to mature.

Chicory and endive can also be included in this section as their growing requirements are much the same as lettuce, but they are a welcome addition to the winter salad bowl, being ready for cutting between January and March. They can have a slightly bitter taste and are best mixed with more traditional salad leaves to add an interesting extra 'bite' to the flavour. 'Blanching' by binding the outer leaves around the plant or covering with a flower pot for three weeks before harvest so no light gets into the crown, will make the flavour more mild. Both endive and chicory should be sown later in the year from mid-April through to August.

Flowerpot Farming

For the same effect in summer, look no further than the spicy tasting rocket varieties: wild, salad and sweet (bearing very attractive flowers if left uncut) which are extremely fast growing. Harvesting the leaves hard back will encourage more to grow. Likewise the 'cut and come again' lettuces such as the 'Red and Green Salad Bowl' and 'Oakleaf' varieties.

Looking after your crop

Being a quick growing vegetable, lettuces like plenty of water to keep them in good condition, and to stop them from running to seed prematurely. Unfortunately, they are also very attractive to slugs and birds, which can be a major nuisance. Slug pellets are effective, but it is far better to use the organic ones which are not harmful to other animals and birds which could eat the affected slugs. Picking off individual slugs when you see them (they are mostly active during the night, so arm yourself with a torch!) will keep the population down, and keeping the area around your lettuces weed-free will deprive them of anywhere else to hide.

Tomatoes

Probably THE vegetable, but more precisely a fruit that we all think of as a vegetable, which springs to most people's minds when they think of container growing, and rightly so. An outdoor variety of tomato will thrive in a large pot, a grow bag or planted straight into the soil. Sowing tomatoes indoors can start in early March andthey can then be planted out after the last frosts.

There are so many varieties to choose from and suited to all different situations. Tiny varieties such as 'Minibel' and 'Totem' for growing on a windowsill, trailing 'Tumbler' for hanging baskets and window boxes, bush varieties (also known in gardener-speak as 'determinate') such as 'Red Alert' and 'Incas F1' – both compact and ideal for containers and cordons (upright varieties), 'Harbinger' – old-fashioned (introduced 1910), with wonderful flavour and 'Golden Sunrise' (a striking golden yellow fruit) . If your plants are eventually going to be growing outside then outdoor types (as above) are recommended, not greenhouse varieties which will need higher temperatures to bear successful crops. Popular ones such as 'Moneymaker' and 'Gardeners Delight', to the more unusual 'Red Brandywine' will give large fruit up to 450g each, thin skinned and very tasty or 'White Beauty', a sweet tasting honey-like flesh, pale yellow skin and very prolific.

Tomatoes are generally high yielding and, in ideal conditions, you should get a good amount of fruit from just two or three plants. The standard time for sowing seed for outdoor tomato varieties is in late March or early April.

Start your plants off from seed on a windowsill indoors in individual pots filled with seed or multi-purpose compost. Cover the seed very lightly with compost and water gently, but well. Place small polythene bags over each pot secured in place with a rubber band. Alternatively, a sheet of glass can be placed across the top of the pots. This is to keep the soil temperature warm and the conditions humid. You should see some signs of life after between 8 and 14 days. Once the seedlings have penetrated the surface the bag or glass can be removed and the plants allowed to grow on until they are about 6-8inches tall. By this time, (hopefully by now late April/early May) the plants will be ready to be hardened off outside, and then transplanted into their growing positions.

Flowerpot Farming

The bush varieties will not require too much attention, just watering regularly to make sure the plants never dry out and feeding with an organic liquid feed once a week during the growing season. They might need staking or a light support if they are in an open position. Cordons, on the other hand, are tall varieties which will definitely need supporting, you will also have to pinch out any side shoots that appear at the base of each leaf where it joins the stem. If you want any more plants, then these shoots can be propagated in a pot of compost and make very healthy growth. Just dip the base of the stem into hormone rooting powder before planting. Cover the pot with a clear polythene bag secured with a rubber band and in 2-3 weeks you will have a rooted new tomato plant!

The main problems you may encounter when growing tomatoes are whitefly (not such a serious problem outdoors), which can be deterred by companion planting some African marigolds ('Tagetes') close by. The strong smelling marigolds are said to put off the whitefly and it has certainly always worked for me, particularly in my polytunnels where these pests usually thrive.

Outdoor grown tomatoes may also suffer from the viral disease blight in a humid, wet summer. The virus is airborne and usually strikes during late July and August. Your plants might not suffer if your garden is tucked away and not close enough to any other tomato or potato growers (potatoes are a close relation and also suffer from blight). Signs include moist looking brown blotches on the leaves, eventually spreading down the stems and onto the ripening fruit. Left unchecked blight will kill the plant, but you can take steps to stop it by removing all the affected leaves. Don't put these leaves in the compost bin or in your wormery – they will be carrying the virus so they need to be disposed of or burned out of harm's way. There are varieties of tomato that have been developed especially to resist blight; a fairly new introduction is 'Ferline'.

Irregular watering can cause the ripening fruits either to split or to show signs of blossom end rot. Blossom end rot affects the bottom of the tomato fruit and looks like a leathery brown patch. Never let the soil completely dry out and water regularly and you shouldn't see either of these conditions.

Cucumber

No salad list would be complete without the cucumber and if you have never tasted one that has been raised outdoors in this country you are in for a pleasant surprise! The bland, watery specimens grown abroad out of season will bear no resemblance to the firm fleshed fruits of 'Marketmore', 'Tanja' or 'Burpless Tasty Green' (don't let the name put you off – it's delicious!) picked from your own garden during the summer. Choose from the outdoor varieties (also known as 'ridge' cucumbers) as these require lower temperatures in which to grow. Outdoor cucumbers normally carry shorter fruits than those grown under glass. Start your seeds off sown in 9cm pots, 2 seeds to a pot, positioned on the windowsill in late spring. Pot the strongest plant into a larger container or pot, then harden off and transplant into a grow bag, large container or pot.

Outdoor cucumbers can be trained over a trellis or up a tall support and will need to be tied in regularly as they grow. This is particularly important once the small cucumbers start forming – they will become quite weighty when they start to fill out and ripen. Few of the problems associated with cucumbers growing inside will affect outdoor varieties. Pests such as red spider mite are indicative of conditions that are too humid, and don't affect plants outside. Pollination concerns that are unique to indoor cucumbers also don't apply to those grown outside, and so long as the soil around the plants is kept well watered and fed with seaweed solution on a weekly basis, by July and August the fruits should be coming thick and fast.

Sweet and Chilli Peppers (Capsicum family)

If you are a pepper fan then growing some of these is a must. There are many compact varieties available that are just perfect for growing in pots and, because they all require a warm, sunny and sheltered position in which to produce crops successfully, being able to move them about is a real bonus. Another option is to plant them up in a grow bag on the patio or balcony – three plants per bag. Very dwarf varieties can even be grown on a sunny windowsill indoors and the foliage and fruit once they start forming look very attractive indeed.

Sweet peppers are the ones with large, blocky fruit; either green, red or yellow. Actually green is the initial colour of the pepper before it changes through into its final colour. The fiery hot chilli peppers are smaller and pointed and either green or red depending on the stage of ripening. Choose from mild to very hot, spicy chillies depending on the strength of your palate!

Pepper seed is best sown in small individual pots of good quality seed or multi-purpose compost in mid to late March. If you sow two seeds per pot, then you can remove the weaker seedling once they emerge which usually takes between two and three weeks, but germination can be erratic so don't give up on them if it takes longer than this. Cover the individual pots with clear polythene bags secured with a rubber band to keep in as much heat and humidity as you can. Likewise, if you are using seed trays, cover with a sheet of glass or cling film which will do the same job. Once the young peppers have around four leaves, plant them into a large pot, and once the roots start to emerge from the bottom, prepare the final pots and containers ready for transplanting. Peppers will definitely need to be acclimatised to outdoor conditions for a week or so before staying outside for good.

During the growing season, keep the plants well watered and feed weekly with a high potash feed such as seaweed liquid or a feed formulated especially for tomatoes. Mulching around the plants will help to stop moisture evaporating in warm weather. In general, peppers are quite healthy plants with regard to pests and diseases and are more likely to be problem prone when grown in greenhouses. However, a poor summer will be detrimental to outdoor peppers (they may not ripen at all), so keep your fingers crossed for hot and sunny conditions and make sure they are in the sunniest position possible. The fruit should be ready for picking from July through to September depending on the variety.

Start picking early fruit regularly as this will stimulate further cropping. Leaving the peppers on the plants to ripen fully is best done later in the season when you have already had an abundant supply.

Dwarf varieties to grow: 'F1 Cheyenne' – a compact chilli pepper (height 45cm) ideal for windowsills and patios, prolific fruiting given good summer conditions. 'Redskin', a true dwarf bell (sweet) pepper for pots and containers, very early fruiting, excellent yields of medium sized red fruits.

Flowerpot Farming

Traditional varieties: 'Bellboy' – a sweet pepper. Excellent and popular, yielding green to red thick walled fruits. 'F1 Krakatoa', a medium sized upright plant producing long slim peppers turning from green to red as they mature. Hot flavour: 'Phoebus', early maturing, with vigorous growth and high yield. Uniform blocky sweet pepper turning from green to yellow and sweet tasting with thick flesh.

If early autumn is approaching, and with it the risk of frost which will be fatal to your peppers and the ripening fruit, you can dig up the entire plant and suspend it in a shed or other frost free environment. The fruits will continue to change colour and should keep in good condition for several weeks.

Spinach and Chard (Leaf Beet)

Included in this list are both the annual spinach and the perpetual spinach, as well as chard in its many colourful guises. These leafy vegetables are worth growing for decorative value alone, but perpetual spinach and Swiss chard will also survive over the winter, allowing you to harvest fresh leaves through the year.

Annual spinach is a short lived plant, and needs to be picked before it runs to seed – which happens fairly quickly during in the summer. Growing it in amongst taller plants to create shade will help prolong its useful life, but it is so fast growing (8-14 weeks from seed to harvest) that you will probably want to sow a row or two every few weeks from mid-March to the end of October for a ready supply. Rich soil containing plenty of organic matter is a must for this vegetable as is regular watering, otherwise the leaves can taste rather bitter. Spinach needs to be sown at a 2.5cm (1" depth) and thinned to about 7.5cm (3") apart once it has germinated. The removed baby leaves can be used in salads.

A less fiddly crop and a much more attractive one are the leaf beets, perpetual spinach and chard. Perpetual spinach is a much sturdier looking plant than its annual counterpart and it lasts much longer – a spring sowing will allow you to harvest leaves from July right through to the following spring if the plants are moved to a sheltered spot in the winter. Any reasonable soil will do but the richer the better. The seeds can be raised indoors and transplanted to be grown in containers outside or directly sown in a raised bed or border in April.

If you are looking for a plant that has decorative qualities as well as being edible, then look no further than chard. Just as easy to grow as its close relative, perpetual spinach, chard is versatile in the kitchen too. If you are using them as attractive features in your border as well as edible ones, then it is better to grow them indoors, then transplant them outside in exactly the spot you want. Swiss, or silver, chard is the standard type, with thick white stalks and white veined leaves, or for even more striking colours look out for Ruby or rhubarb chard (bright red stems and red veins against dark green leaves) and the variety 'Bright Lights' which comes in a myriad of colours: red, yellow, orange, white and green stemmed. The foliage of all varieties can be used like spinach and the thick fleshy stalks can be removed and steamed like asparagus.

Chard and perpetual spinach need a bit more room than ordinary spinach so aim for individual plants in containers with smaller vegetables growing around them or in rows spaced about 30cm (1ft) apart if planted in a raised bed or in the kitchen garden.

You can pick the leaves to eat as soon as they are large

Flowerpot Farming

enough, making sure to cut them off well above the growing point in the ground rather than pulling up the whole plant. Lots more leaves will develop in their place.

Brassicas

Brassicas are a wide-ranging vegetable family, extremely productive and generally very hardy. The family includes cabbages, Brussels sprouts, kale, broccoli, cauliflowers, turnips and, surprisingly, even radishes and turnips which obviously don't look anything like cabbages, but the fact that they are closely related means you will need to include them in with the brassicas if you are rotating your crops each year to keep the soil healthy.

Because they are such hardy vegetables, brassicas can be sown in-situ in early spring as well as indoors in trays for transplanting later. They need to be sown about ½" deep (this applies across the whole brassica spectrum) The first ones to sow are the spring cabbages such as 'Greyhound', a pointed cabbage and a traditional favourite. Another very early cabbage is 'Golden Acre', a densely leaved round variety. Most brassicas are best growing in borders because they take up a fair amount of space, but dwarf varieties such as Kale 'dwarf curled' are ideal in a container and of course other varieties can be used as baby leaves before they even reach maturity so you can grow them in a smaller space. A striking kale is the strap leafed variety, 'Black Tuscany', very delicious steamed or in stir fries. Cauliflowers have a reputation for being one of the trickier members of the cabbage family to grow, but given a rich soil and good moisture levels, very good results can be obtained when grown in deep containers or raised beds.

Following on for sowing later in spring, Savoy and red

cabbages, broccoli and Brussels sprouts can all be started off in April or earlier if you are following the windowsill method.

Radishes and Turnips

The fastest growing brassica is the radish, closely followed by the turnip. You can have fully grown radishes in as little as 3 weeks from a sowing made during the summer. Turnips take a little longer but it is possible to harvest tender baby roots within 6 weeks. These are great vegetables to grow if you are really struggling for space as they will make way for other crops to be planted once they are harvested. If you like eating them enough to want a continual crop or radishes from late spring through to autumn, then sowing short rows every three or four weeks from mid-March until late August will give you a plentiful supply.

Kohl Rabi

An underrated and overlooked member of the brassica family is the kohl rabi, doubly useful in the kitchen because both its leaves and its swollen stem (which makes it look like a root vegetable) can be eaten. Everything but the root itself can be used. The young leaves can be boiled or steamed like spinach, the globes braised, boiled, steamed or used in soups, or it can be used raw, grated onto salads. It has a delicate, nutty flavour. Kohl rabi is easy to grow and striking to see when it is growing, particularly the deep red variety 'F1 Blaro'. A pale green one called 'F1 Lanro' is also available. Kohl rabi can be harvested when quite small and tender or can be left until the swollen stem is slightly larger than a golf ball.

Flowerpot Farming

Legumes

Peas

Although they are not the easiest of vegetables to get a good crop from, the comparison between the fresh, sweet taste of home-grown peas and anything bought fresh or frozen is worlds apart, and even if yields are small peas can be eaten straight off the plant – such a delicacy! It is possible to grow a succession of crops for harvesting from May/June through to the autumn. Mangetout and sugar snap peas are just as tasty when home grown and freshly picked, but are usually sown just once during April and May for picking in August and September.

It is possible to grow peas in containers; you might want to stick to the dwarf varieties that need little in the way of support, or you may want to grow the plants up a wigwam or other structure. Plants can be as little as 45cm (18") tall, or up to 120cm (4ft) for the larger ones.

Seed can be sown direct where they are to grow in containers, in outdoor soil beds, or indoors in pots to be transplanted later. Mice are very partial to pea seed and young seedlings, and sometimes the whole of an outdoor sown crop can be completely destroyed. Transplanting out older plants is a safer bet if there are mice around.

Beans

The bean family is a large one and you could argue that there is a variety to suit every situation in a small space garden.

The dwarf French bean is ideal for small containers and

window boxes and, unlike the climbing French bean, it makes a nice compact plant about 30cm-38cm (12-15") high. Aim to keep them well watered and they will be happy. The seeds are fairly large and can be sown indoors from April-early May in small pots or in-situ from mid-May to July where you want them to grow. Germination will take a week or two. Good varieties to look for are 'F1 Safari' (a round, pencil podded type) and 'The Prince', a popular flat pod type; these are both high yielding and hardy varieties. After hardening them off for a week or so, plant them into their final containers once the risk of frost has passed (from mid-May depending on how far north you live). You could be harvesting your French beans from July to mid-October dependent on when they were sown and which varieties they are.

A few varieties of French beans are climbers and will reach heights of between 1.8-2.5m (6-7ft). Similar to their dwarf relations, they also produce both flat podded and pencil podded crops, and can be planted up in containers provided they can be given some support via netting, trellis or a traditional wigwam. Their requirements are simple; in reasonably fertile soil, all they will need is regular watering. When the plants have started to produce pods, pick them regularly to keep them producing more – if any beans are missed and reach maturity (knobbly, tough and stringy beans), bean production will cease.

Climbing varieties: 'Hunter', 'Limka' and 'Festival'.

Runner Beans

The giants of the bean world, runner beans are capable of producing very significant quantities of beans from August to October. If you have experienced the disappointment of shop bought runner beans that turned out stringy and inedible, then picking and eating your own home grown ones will be a revelation. Commercially grown beans are generally harvested when they have grown too large (and tough) but you will be able to pick yours when they are still young and tender.

Runner beans can eventually climb up to 3.5m (10ft), so will need some sort of tall and sturdy support. Traditionally they have been trained up wigwams made from bamboo canes or up a series of crossed canes tied at the apex to horizontal cross pieces. For great features in the garden they can also be trained to climb up a trellis or netting on a wall or up an arch or pergola. The dense foliage and flowers are very eye-catching during the summer, and provide useful shade if wanted, over a seating area or bower seat.

Because they need deep, rich, fertile soil that provides plenty of nutrients for them to grow rapidly, runner beans are best grown in vegetable borders or beds, raised beds and large, deep containers. Half wooden barrels are ideal, big enough to allow you to be able to incorporate a wigwam support that the beans can climb up. A good quantity of organic matter mixed into the compost will add fertility and increase moisture retaining properties. Mulching around the plants once they are established is also recommended.

Runner beans are tender vegetables, so seed can be left until late April or early May before sowing indoors (for planting out late May through until mid-June). Compared to other vegetable seeds these are HUGE and can be sown in individual pots. Expect to see the seedlings break the soil surface in about 7-10 days. The young plants should be hardened off once they are about 15cm-20cm (6-8") tall, then planted in a container or direcly into the ground outside. The supports should already be in place, ready for your beans to climb up.

Initially it is a good idea to loosely tie in the plants to the supports – this will encourage them to start twining and climbing up on their own.

If you are sowing outside, then a late May/early June sowing is recommended. By then the risk of frost will have passed. Ideally, the soil can be prepared the previous autumn, and to help the soil retain water a good quantity of manure of compost can be dug in, and this will have had time to settle down by the time you are ready to sow the following year.

Before sowing outside, set up your bean supports; then you can sow each bean in exactly the right place close to an upright. The beans need to be sown at about a 5cm (2") depth, and about 45cm (8") apart.

Keep the plants well watered throughout the growing season, and pinch out the tops when they have reached the top of your supports. Depending on when you planted them, picking the pods will start in earnest from late July onwards – to ensure continued cropping it is vital that you pick every one; if just one pod is left on to mature it will trigger the reproduction cycle to stop and there will be no more beans. Luckily, runner beans can be frozen, made into chutney or distributed amongst your neighbours.

Broad Beans

On the whole, broad beans are a pretty easy crop to grow, although they do prefer a rich, moist soil and plenty of room for their roots to grow which makes them a bit of a challenge in a container. They are definitely worth the effort, though, because if conditions are right, you should get a very good crop of tasty beans and what's more, the bean tops are delicious too, steamed and served with butter. The dwarf varieties, approximately 30cm (12") high, are the better bet for contained growing or for exposed sites. The taller ones (up to 4ft or more) are suited to outside raised beds and borders as they will require supporting with sticks.

Broad bean varieties are classified in three groups:

Longpods: not surprisingly these bear long narrow pods. They are generally the hardiest, better yielding and earliest. They include varieties for autumn sowing as well as spring. 'Aquadulce', tall and prolific, good for freezing, 'Imperial Green Longpod', 5-8 beans per pod, excellent for freezing and with a very good flavour.

Windsors: 'Imperial Green Windsor', high yielding with an excellent flavour and later maturing.
'Scorpio' with a good flavour and texture and heavy cropping with small to medium sized beans.

Dwarf: 'The Sutton', deservedly popular and widely available. 45cm in height. For autumn and spring sowing. 'Medes', not a true dwarf, but a compact variety with an RHS Award for Garden Merit and a heavy yield of medium size pods with 5-6 beans in each.

Being pretty hardy and requiring little heat for germination, broad beans can actually be sown in the autumn, although this can sometimes be a bit of a risk because, if the winter is a particularly wet one or you live in a cold area, the seeds may rot. However, you do get an earlier crop if this is successful (early June onwards). Most direct sowing is carried out from March to late May – if you want a succession of beans from July to September you can sow a few each month. If you are starting your seed off indoors in pots, then you

Flowerpot Farming is about maximising space but with thought it can be decorative as well as functional. The extra bonus is that it's great for wildlife too!

Using a tower made from old tyres gives depth.

Chillis work well in pots - both indoors or in a sunny position outside.

Give the view from your window a fresh and tasty look.

Raised beds are excellent for increasing your variety of crops.

The variety of lettuce you can grow will equal that of any supermarket shelf.

Garden centres are
well stocked but
don't just stick to
the conventional. As
long as the pot has
drain holes most
containers will do.

Runner beans wil climb up virtually anything making them great for using up wall space.

Squashes, on the other hand, obey the laws of gravity!

Strawberries are
easy to grow in pots
and raised beds
- even in hanging
baskets!

You can have a mini orchard with trees planted in barrels.

Old Buckets, traditional flowerpots and even tin cans can be adapted for use.

Enjoy!

can sow them as early as February for hardening off and transplanting during March. The recommended depth for sowing either in pots or direct is 5cm (2") and 20cm (8") apart for each plant. Once the plants are flowering and the first young beans can be seen towards the base, the tops can be removed. These will make a tasty meal, but the tops should be pinched out anyway to deter a common pest of broad beans – blackfly. The tender tops are a favourite place for blackfly to live.

Harvesting

Beans can be picked when the pods are still small and immature to be cooked and eaten whole, otherwise harvested larger and shelled. Shelled beans should have a green 'scar' (where they were attached to the pod); if this is brown, the bean will be tough and leathery no matter how long you cook it!

Pests and diseases

Apart from blackfly, mice and slugs can also damage broad bean crops. Mice, in particular, can dig up and eat autumn sown seed and emerging seedlings. This can also happen in spring, but the longer over-wintering period poses a greater risk. Slugs are partial to the young plants, especially in damp conditions if the area around is not kept weeded which gives them plenty of places to hide.

The Squash Family

This group of plants includes marrows, courgettes, pumpkins, and the brightly coloured and unusually shaped summer and winter squash varieties. None of

97

this family could honestly be described as compact plants but most of them are highly productive and just three or four plants could easily keep you in courgettes, marrows or squashes throughout the summer onwards, depending on which varieties you grow. Squashes are an example of one of the very good reasons to start growing your own vegetables. If you've only ever seen traditional green courgettes or the only squashes you are able to buy in the shops are cobnuts, then you are in for a treat. As well as the usual dark green courgettes,('F1 Early Gem', 'Zucchini'), seeds for a courgette producing pale green fruit, 'F1 Opal', yellow fruit, F1 Goldrush", round green fruit, 'F1 Eight Ball' and round yellow fruit, 'F1 One Ball' are available to the home farmer.

All squashes are tender and won't tolerate any degree of frost so they need to be sown and planted in the vegetable season. Luckily they mature very quickly once they are established, taking 10-14 weeks from seed to harvest. Squash seeds are large and flat and easy to handle and are best sown about 2cm deep into small pots indoors in late April/early May, or outside in a container or in the garden from May onwards. Transplant your pots to wherever you want them to grow outside towards the end of May through early June, not forgetting to harden them off for a couple of weeks beforehand.

Courgettes are the most popular of this group and form slightly more compact plants with a 60-90cm spread and about 45cm high. Given the right growing conditions and provided you keep cutting the fruits to encourage the formation of more, you will get 20 or more courgettes per plant over a long period. Leaving some of the fruits on the plant to grow into marrow will slow down the production of new courgettes, but if you want to harvest the odd marrow and have no room for a marrow variety this may be the solution for you.

If you like your marrows to come with traditional stripes, then choose a 'proper' marrow variety. There are both trailing and slightly more compact 'bush' varieties available. Trailing ones can look striking if grown over walls – the large, spiky leaves and vivid yellow flowers are very attractive in their own right and that is even before the fruits start to appear along the length of the stem. 'Long Green Trailing' has been around for years and, as its name suggests, will trail along the ground for several feet, 'F1 Zebra cross' is a bush type and very high yielding with well-marked stripes. A new variety called 'F1 Bush Baby' is a more compact plant producing smaller sized marrows (about ¾ of the size of a standard marrow). Because of this, it is ideal for container cultivation.

Summer Squash

Strictly speaking, both marrows and courgettes come under this section too, being summer cropping varieties that have a reasonably short 'shelf life', i.e. needing to be eaten with a week or so after picking. However, there are also a few closely related varieties, not often seen but well worth growing for a touch of the unusual and a splash of colour both in the garden and on the dinner plate. These are the summer squashes which include the 'patty pan' varieties, scalloped edged fruits in a varied array of colours. They are rapid growers with the majority taking only 45-50 days to mature. 'F1 Moonbeam' (pale green/white skin), 'F1 Sunbeam' (golden yellow skin) and 'F1 Total Eclipse' (dark green). All varieties can be sliced and cooked like courgettes or roasted whole in the oven

Another unusual member of this group is the spaghetti marrow or vegetable spaghetti. This will produce fruits up to 1.2kg in weight. These can be boiled, baked, or steamed whole. The cooked flesh forms ribbons, similar in appearance to spaghetti, with a slightly sweet flavour.

Winter Squash

This diverse group of vegetables includes the giant pumpkin right down to the comparatively small butternut squash.

Pumpkins need no introduction, and you might have decided straight away that they are much too large to be any use in a small space. However, as well as the monster varieties bred to produce competition sized pumpkins, there are a few 'baby' ones that are great for both decorative and culinary purposes, so don't discount them altogether; the bright orange pumpkins can create visual impact in a small space as well as producing the raw materials for pumpkin pie! 'Munchkin', which has fruits weighing only 125g each, and 'Baby Bear', bearing slightly larger 1kg pumpkins, are worth looking out for.

There are many other winter squashes to choose from and what a wide-ranging lot they are! From spotted, striped, green, orange, yellow and red in colour and in a myriad of different shapes, the majority are very useful in the kitchen and have a long storage life if kept in cool, dry conditions. At the time of writing in March, I still have a Turk's Turban squash in good condition that was harvested the previous October. Some plants are of compact habit and some will trail so there is a squash for every situation and requirement.

Cultivation instructions are the same as for marrows, courgettes and pumpkins. Winter squash varieties generally take a few weeks longer to mature but should still be harvested before the first frosts. Store somewhere cool and dry and your squash crops will last for months. Just the thing for making delicious soups and for roasting over the winter months.

The butternut squash is the most likely type you will find in the supermarkets; very occasionally you might see the excellent culinary variety 'Harlequin'. But how about 'Crown Prince', a grey skinned variety with bright orange flesh, or the gem squash 'Rolet' producing tennis ball sized dark green fruits (trailing), or the aptly named 'Turk's Turban', a very ornamental, but edible large striped orange, green and white fruit? A quick look in one seed catalogue at the time of writing and I noted 14 different varieties of butternut and various other winter squash.

Root Vegetables

Carrots

Is there really anyone who doesn't like carrots? Usually one of the only vegetables that children will eat, it is possible to grow them in a raised bed, a deepish container or of course in your vegetable beds or in a flower border. The feathery leaves create an attractive fern-like backdrop for other vegetables and flowers and take up little room. If you choose to grow one of the shorter 'stump rooted' ('Nantes' type) or a round rooted variety, then you can get away with growing them in containers. Carrots usually take anywhere between 12 and 24 weeks from sowing to maturity – but if you like sweet, baby carrots, they can be harvested once they reach the size you require (another bonus of growing your own crops). As well as the familiar orange carrots, there are also yellow and red varieties.

There are two groups of carrots; earlies and maincrops. Earlies mature from 12-18 weeks, maincrops take up to 24 weeks. The early types tend to be sweeter and are mostly used straight after harvesting but some varieties do keep longer. You can sow early carrots at regular intervals all through the growing season if you want to and, as they are reasonably quick to mature, you will be able to pick them over a long period. Maincrop carrots have generally longer and larger roots, which means that because they take longer to dry out in storage, they keep better. They are not as sweet tasting as earlies, but you can store them for several months.

An old method of storing carrots (and in fact other root vegetables) is by storing them in dry sand or peat in a large wooden box or tray. The ideal time for this is in October using a maincrop variety of carrot. Only use sound carrots (cut the leaves off ½" above the crown) – damaged ones should be used straight away because they will be very likely to rot. Place a 5cm (2") layer of sand or peat in the bottom of the box then place each carrot carefully side by side but not touching and cover with more sand or peat, repeating the process until the box is full or you have used up all your carrots. Store the box in a dry place and the carrots should keep until March. It is a good idea to check now and again to make sure that none have started to rot – if left like this it could spread to the whole crop.

Carrots are one of the few vegetables that cannot be transplanted; they need to be sown right where they are to stay until harvest. The soil needs to be light, fertile, well drained and free of stones. If you are going to dig in mature compost or manure, this needs to be done several months before the seed is sown – in stony or freshly composted/manured soil, carrots have a tendency to 'fork' (become misshapen).

Carrot seed is tiny and needs to be sown into a very fine seedbed in a shallow drill, not too deep or thickly (this will save you time thinning the young plants out later). The surrounding soil needs to be kept weed free at all times so that the young seedlings will not encounter any competition. Carrots can be a little erratic when germinating – especially if the weather outside takes a turn for the worse – but expect to see signs of growth in about 18 days.

Thin out your crop, trying to aim for carrots about 5cm (2") apart so they have plenty of room to grow, but be careful to dispose of all the small carrot plants you pull out well away from the remaining ones left in the row and firm down the soil around the plants because a major pest, carrot root fly, could well be attracted to your crop by the smell of the bruised leaves (carrot leaves have that distinctive 'carroty' odour). Carrot root fly maggots can completely ruin a crop by eating their way through the roots and eventually killing the whole plant. An important point to note is that these insects cannot fly above 60cm (2ft), so an effective preventative measure could be to erect a 60cm barrier of horticultural fleece around your carrots so the flies can't get to them.

Fortunately you shouldn't encounter too many other problems with carrots, just make sure they are kept well watered in dry spells. Split roots can occur if heavy rain occurs after a prolonged dry period and sometimes you might see a few carrots with green tops. These are caused by sunlight but the carrots' eating qualities aren't affected.

Flowerpot Farming

Beetroot

Still one of our most underrated vegetables, it seems that beetroot is something that people seem to either love or hate which is a pity. Perhaps this is because of unpleasant childhood memories of picked beetroot in vinegar, but this deeply coloured root vegetable can be used in so many other ways that it is a pity to discount it simply because of this. Beetroot can also be roasted or boiled and eaten either hot or cold, grated raw, in chutneys and the young leaves can be cooked just like spinach so nothing should get wasted.

There are also different types of beetroot to choose from. Different shapes and colours are available, although you probably wouldn't think so judging by the standard round burgundy red specimens in the shops. Yes, as well as the round ones, some beetroot varieties are cylindrical, others long and tapered and colours vary from white 'Albina Ice', golden 'Burpees Golden', red/white striped (alternately coloured sections through the root) 'Chioggia', and, of course, varying shades of medium red to the deepest maroon 'Bikores' and the ever-popular 'Boltardy'.

The roots can be harvested when young as baby beets, or left to mature to tennis ball size. The small, round beets are great for container growing as they take up little room and can be ready for picking a couple of months after sowing. If you want to keep them in the soil longer, they will happily grow on for several weeks more and the bolt resistant varieties in particular should hold well in the ground without running to seed for a considerably longer period so long as you keep them well watered throughout. Beetroots can be sown from April to July and the quick maturing globe varieties are ideal for sowing little and often (every 2-3 weeks or so) over this time then you won't get a glut all maturing at the same time.

The beetroot 'seed' itself looks small and wrinkled, but is in fact a cluster containing several seeds. Modern developments have produced what is known as a 'monogerm' seed, which will produce only one plant rather than the chance of several from the standard seed. This type of seed is useful if you don't want the bother of thinning out, but to be honest, if you are aiming to harvest the beets in their early stages of growth, then they won't require so much room and you will get more baby beetroot for your money. Best sown where they are to crop, beetroot does not take kindly to being transplanted, so bury the seed about 1.4 cm (¾") under the surface of a reasonably fertile soil or compost. If you really must sow them indoors, then use module trays which will minimise root disturbance when they are eventually moved to their new site.

Spacing for mature beet is ideally 7.5cm (3") apart but for mini-beet you can space considerably closer. Keep the soil around the plants weeded and don't let them dry out throughout the season and your beetroot will be perfectly happy.

Parsnips

Parsnips aren't difficult to grow given the right conditions, but they hate to be transplanted or have their roots restricted (as in containers) and in the main are really only suited to growing either in raised beds or in vegetable plots and borders. Having said that, however, there are some recent introductions of dwarf parsnip varieties which can be grown in containers over 25cm (10") in depth. These can be harvested when immature, at about 14 weeks from sowing and around finger thickness. 'Arrow' and 'Lancer' are shorter rooted and ideal for restricted growing and early harvesting.

Parsnip seed needs to be sown directly into light, well drained soil that is free of stones and with a reasonable level of fertility. Stony soil can cause the roots to grow into odd shapes and/or several shoots which are time-consuming to prepare for cooking. Germination can be slow and erratic, and in heavy soils not very successful if planted before the soil warms up sufficiently in late spring. For early harvested roots the seed can be sown fairly closely, thinning to about 8cm (3") per plant. Mature crops will need thinning to between 15-20cm (6-8") apart.

Parsnips in containers will need regular watering but with crops outside this is only necessary during prolonged dry spells to prevent the soil from drying out completely.
Carrot root fly can sometimes be attracted to parsnips, but this is not usually a serious problem. In dry conditions, a disease called canker can penetrate through the tops of the roots if they crack. This normally only happens with larger specimens and regularly watering should ensure that any cracking of the crown doesn't occur in the first place.

The roots should be ready for harvesting from September right through the winter and they are best left in the ground until they are needed because this will keep them in excellent condition. The effect of frost on the buried roots really does improve their flavour. If you prefer to dig them out before this, however, they can also be stored in boxes of sand in the same way as for carrots and beetroot.

Potatoes

Potatoes are easy to grow and once they are planted there is little you have to do except water them in dry conditions and wait in anticipation! They are normally ready for harvesting once the plants have flowered. You can always check underneath the soil to see if the tubers are ready for lifting and, if not, carefully cover them over again and wait a bit longer.

Potatoes should be grown from certified seed potatoes. These are specially raised for the purpose of raising new crops and will be disease free, which cannot always be guaranteed if you save tubers yourself from your previous year's crop. Seed potatoes can be bought via mail order or garden centres. Some garden centres sell them loose by weight, which is ideal if you only want a few potatoes to grow. The best time to buy them is in late winter (January/February).

You will come across two terms that are used to describe the main growing types: earlies and maincrops. This simply refers to how long each group takes to produce a mature crop – you don't necessarily have to plant the earlies any earlier than the maincrops, you will just be harvesting them quicker, but maincrops will store better for longer. Earlies take between 75 and 110 days to harvest, maincrops 135 to 160 days. There are lots of varieties, both new introductions and heirlooms, of differing shapes and colours.

Before you plant your potatoes they will need to be 'chitted', particularly the early varieties, although modern thinking considers that this is not really necessary for the maincrops. (You don't see farmers chitting their potatoes before planting or carefully setting them in the soil shoots upwards!) All this simply means is starting off the tubers indoors, then inducing them to produce shoots before they are planted. The best way to do this is to place the seed potatoes on a shallow tray – an old egg box is ideal because it will hold the tubers in place – 'rose' end up (the part of the potato with the most 'eyes'). Then they need to be stored in a cool, dry, light place in order for the shoots to develop. Once the shoots are around 2.5cm (1") long the seed potatoes are ready to be planted, but if shoot growth is still minimal in mid/late March, don't be too worried; sometimes this does happen. You can still plant them as they are.

For cultivating your potatoes on a patio in containers, see the project in Chapter 5.

Traditionally, potato growing is done on a big scale with each individual plant taking up a lot of room, but this is not at all necessary if you can't spare the space. A simple way to get a crop of potatoes is by planting a couple of tubers (with the shoots facing upwards) in a very large pot or bucket with drainage holes in the bottom. Fill this half way up with multi-purpose compost with a bit of manure or home produced compost mixed in. Place the tubers on the surface and cover with a further 2" layer of compost. As the shoots break the soil surface, add more compost, eventually reaching near the top of the container. You can use whatever variety you choose, but a first early is probably the best for confined growing as the crop will then most likely be ready before the hot months of July and August arrive and constant watering is necessary.

Pests and diseases

Surprisingly, because one is primarily thought of as a root vegetable and the other as a fruit produced on a stem, you wouldn't think that potatoes belonged to the same family group of vegetables as tomatoes, but they do. If you grow both of them you will see that their foliage is very similar, and if left longer than normal before harvesting, potato plants will eventually develop tiny green fruit similar to little tomatoes. Why I'm telling you this is so that you are aware that potatoes are also very susceptible to blight, a very common and serious disease of both vegetables that spreads rapidly. The good news, particularly for potatoes, is that blight doesn't usually take a great hold on crops until July onwards – so if you are growing the early varieties, with luck your potatoes will be out of the ground by the end of June. Blight is an airborne virus which usually starts spreading in warm moist summers. Look out for brown blotches on the leaves that spread down onto the stems. Eventually the blight spores will get washed down into the soil too, rotting the tubers under the ground. Although there is no remedy for blight, all will not be lost if you spot it early enough. If only the leaves are affected it is worth checking under the soil to see if the still healthy tubers are of a useful size for eating. If they are then dig them up immediately. Alternatively, the foliage can be completely removed, burnt and destroyed (never put diseased leaves on your compost heap). After waiting about 3 weeks, the tubers can then be lifted and will be okay for long term storage; the blight spores that affected the soil surface will have died by then.

The big bonus of growing your own potato crop is that you will be able to choose from numerous varieties of common, traditional and heirloom varieties, the majority of which are not grown by farmers and therefore never make it into the shops. Certain varieties have fallen out of favour over the years, often just because they are less easy to cultivate on a large, commercial scale and as more disease resistant cultivars are introduced. Seed merchants via mail order and some good garden centres offer many different varieties you won't often see.

Flowerpot Farming

A small selection of potatoes varieties:

Edzell Blue: a striking blue/purple potato, very floury and suitable for steaming which makes good mashed potato. An old Victorian variety, a second early and ready from July to August.

Maris Bard: First introduced in 1972, this was the earliest cropping potato at that time but has now been pre-empted by newer varieties. It is a good all-rounder for cooking, is high yielding and the tubers are of a good size.

Home Guard: as the name suggests, introduced during WWII (1942 to be precise). Another early variety producing good crops of tubers. Still a favourite of many gardeners.

Rocket: A first early and a fairly recent variety. Very popular and seed potatoes are easy to find in most garden centres/seed merchants. Extremely high yields of good sized, smooth, attractive tubers.

Charlotte: A second early salad potato with nice, waxy textured flesh when cooked. Very reliable with a reasonable resistance to blight – particularly the tubers. Among the best flavoured salad potatoes.

Red Duke of York: a vigorous variety, producing large, red-skinned tubers and an attractive green/red foliage. A first early with a wonderful flavour.

Pink Fir Apple: a very old variety from 1850. The gourmet's potato with a fine flavour, the long tubers have an unusual knobbly appearance. Cooking them whole makes preparation much easier! A late maincrop, so ready from September onwards.

Outdoor potatoes can be given more room and planted at up to 10cm (4") deep and 30cm (12") between plants. Potatoes love well manured, rich soil. Organic fertiliser can be also be worked into the soil at the time of planting or scattered around on the surface during the growing season. As the foliage emerges earth up around the plants to about 15cm (6"). This ensuresthat none of the tubers closest to the surface will be turned green (and rendered inedible and poisonous). Earlies are normally ready for digging up once the flowers have opened and maincrops should be lifted when the foliage has turned brown and withered (not to be confused with blight symptoms: natural dying off of potato tops leaves dry and crispy remains of foliage – blight is normally much earlier and the brown patches have a much 'wetter' look to them and may have a white fringe of mould in damp weather). Lift in late August if you are planning to use the tubers immediately. If they are for storage, then delay digging them up until September or early October, when they will store much better. Choose a dry day to do this and let the potatoes dry on the soil surface for a few hours. The best way to store them is in hessian or brown paper sacks in a cool, dry place away from the risk of frost. They should last until spring.

Alliums

Onions

Where would we be without onions? You might argue that in small spaces, onions, so plentiful and cheap to buy in the shops, are really not worth allocating a precious growing space to. However, I would urge you to grow them just for one season – and from sets (immature bulbs) which take 20 weeks to mature rather than the

Flowerpot Farming

lengthy 46 weeks you would have to wait if you grew them from seed. They are extremely easy vegetables and store very well given the right conditions. Home grown onions always seem to be much hotter than the mild flavoured Spanish onions bought in the shops so you can use them sparingly or not, according to taste! Shallots, which produce lots of smaller onions from one bulb and which are normally used for pickling, garnishing or cooking are cultivated in exactly the same way.

Onion sets (and shallot sets) can be purchased from garden centres any time from early February to April. Some places sell the sets loose by weight so if you only want to fill a small area you can buy just a few. Sets don't need such fine soil for planting and although a fertile one is required, too much recently incorporated organic matter will be detrimental to bulb growth (the leaves will develop instead of the bulb itself). Better to fertilise the year before. Plant the sets by pushing them gently into soft soil leaving the tips just above the surface, about 10cm (4") apart for onions, 15cm (6") for shallots, to allow them more room to spread.

If the onions are in open ground you might have a problem with birds trying to pull them out, so cover them with netting if this is likely. All your onion crop requires from now on is to be kept weed free as this can affect the yield; also keep an eye out to make sure the sets aren't lifted by birds or late frosts – push them back into the soil if they are. Give them some water only if the soil really dries out (this will help them swell and prevent running to seed prematurely) then just watch them grow. Once the bulbs have swelled sufficiently they are ready to harvest. They can be eaten immediately or if you want to save some for storage, dig them up and leave them on the surface to dry for a week or two if the weather is dry – or indoors spread out on a tray if not.

Store your onions in an onion net (you can recycle one that has previously had onions in it) or in trays or even strung together to be suspended in a cool, well lit, dry place and they should keep until late spring.

Reliable varieties include: 'Bedfordshire Champion' (popular, good keeping qualities, large), 'Red Baron' (red onion, strong flavoured, nice change from white varieties), 'Sturon' (excellent for storage, large round yellow-brown skin, a favourite reliable choice).

Shallots: 'Red Sun' (large round bulbs with reddish brown skin and good flavour. Good in storage – requires later planting than other varieties, no earlier than March).
'Longor' (a traditional French shallot with elongated bulbs. Mild flavoured).

Spring Onions

Unlike ordinary onions, these are quick to grow (12 weeks from sowing to harvest) and to get a succession of spring onions through the summer you should sow a row or so every 3 weeks from early spring through to the autumn. Relatively undemanding to grow, they are always grown from seed and can be raised in containers and raised beds as well as in a vegetable patch or garden border.

Spring onions transplant well and you can start them off indoors in a seed tray or module tray. For easy cultivation, sowing in module trays means you can sow as many as 4 or 5 seeds per module and simply plant the whole lot together in a group when you are transplanting them outside. Once they are big enough for picking, you will have a ready-made bunch! The seeds can also be directly sown in outside soil in shallow drills in finely prepared soil. Aim to space each seed about ½" apart which will give it plenty of room, but don't worry too much if they are closer than that; you can always pull the odd one out for harvest, leaving the remainder wider apart to grow on a little more.

I have found that keeping the plants well watered throughout tends to make the flavour milder, but others that I have forgotten to look after and that have dried out have much more 'bite' to them – great if you like a strong tasting onion!

Varieties: 'White Lisbon', 'Ramrod'.

Leeks

Leeks really are an easy crop – but they are also a long term one. Sown during March and April, they will be ready for lifting some time between October and the following March, depending on whether the variety you are growing is an early or late, maturing at respectively 30 and 45 weeks. Of course they can be grown as baby vegetables and this method of cultivation is probably best for containers and raised beds where space will be at a premium. Once the young leek plants reach the desired size (as small as you wish), they can be picked and will be very tender and delicious.

If you can give them a bit more time to grow and reach mature size, then they can remain in the ground for several months until they are needed. A great bonus of this is that they will be ready for picking at a time of year when very few other types of fresh vegetable are still about. Leeks prefer a nutrient rich soil full of humus, so digging in organic compost or well rotted manure the previous autumn will be required to help you harvest bumper crops.

Leeks can be sown in seed trays (I usually sow them in modules, one seed per cell, which makes eventually planting them out much easier) indoors in early March or April. However, if you are going to eat them as baby leeks you can sow 3 or 4 per module and then transplant in a group rather than as single plants. This will require much less effort and a larger crop of leeks in a smaller space! Wait until May until you transfer them into their final containers. Use the same method of planting the young leek plants into 15cm (6") deep holes – this will blanch the lower stem, giving that authentic leek look.

If you're growing them in a raised bed or outside in your garden then they can be sown direct outside, from mid-March or later. The soil needs to be worked into a fine tilth as leek (and onion, for that matter) seed is fairly small. Sow very thinly in rows 15cm (6") apart. Germination, either indoors in trays or outside, will take between 14-18 days. Even with outdoor sown leeks, it is better to transplant them into their final positions once they are about the thickness of a pencil because they need to be planted much deeper in order to create the white 'blanched' effect on the lower shank of the leek. Carefully ease the small leeks out of their nursery bed with a dibber or trowel, trying not to damage the delicate roots. Prepare the new growing site and make 15cm holes with a dibber 15cm apart and 30cm between rows. Drop a leek plant into each hole and gently water it in to settle it into place – don't fill the soil back into the hole.

After this there is very little you will have to do to keep your leek crop growing on happil, apart from keeping the weeds down and applying water regularly to those grown in containers and raised beds.

Flowerpot Farming

Garlic

Although not a true member of the onion family, garlic is grown in a similar way and produces edible bulbs. It should also be included in the same rotation. Each garlic bulb used for planting is divided into individual cloves that are planted and new plants formed from each one. It is possible to use garlic you have bought from a supermarket to grow more yourself, but it is much better to buy specially raised stock for planting supplied by specialist companies and mail order seed merchants. Then you will know exactly what variety you are growing and be totally sure that the bulbs are free of disease. Bulbs aren't cheap to buy initially, but you can always keep some back to plant yourself the following year.

Garlic needs a well drained soil, and not one that has recently had manure added to it. It will grow on a heavier soil, but you will need to plant the cloves less deeply. Preferably a sunny, warm site is best, but this is a vegetable that will be at home almost anywhere. It has a fairly shallow root system and you should be able to get away with a soil depth of around 6". There are garlic varieties for both autumn and spring planting but both will mature in mid to late summer. Garlic appreciates a long growing period, and generally the autumn plant types are larger and juicier than the spring sown. Plant each clove pointed end upwards around 7.5cm (3") deep in light soil, but only 2.5cm (1") deep in heavy clay. They can be spaced as little as 7.5cm/3" apart, but if you can give them more space, the bigger they will grow.

The growing plants will need regular weeding and watering in dry weather. When garlic is ready for harvesting, the leaves will start to turn yellow. The new bulbs are formed underground so you will have to lift them carefully out of the soil. Try not to damage them as this will affect their storage life. As with onions, if the weather is dry just leave the lifted garlic on the surface for about a week, or indoors if it turns wet.

Dried garlic for storage always looks very attractive tied into plaits; alternatively, store it in wooden boxes in cool, dry conditions. Some long keeping strains will last for up to 12 months.

Recommended varieties: 'Thermidrome', 'Cristo' and 'Solent Wight'.

Sweetcorn

One of the most rewarding plants for the home farmer really has to be this one. Admittedly, sweetcorn is not one of the easiest vegetables to grow, especially in confined conditions, and will need careful siting to ensure the plants are in the best position to produce one or more cobs each, but once you have tasted fresh sweetcorn picked from your own garden, nothing less will do. Harvested and then immediately cooked (or eaten raw, if you prefer), it will be the juiciest and sweetest you have ever tasted.

Sweetcorn is a tall plant and can reach up to 4-6 feet. It also has a very striking look and would make an impact at the back of any sunny border. Try to site sweetcorn where it will receive full sun but be protected from the wind. It really does need a good summer to yield a good crop, but new and improved varieties especially bred for the Northern hemisphere and for difficult growing conditions are frequently introduced.

Sweetcorn is pollinated by pollen falling from the tassel-

Flowerpot Farming

like flowers at the very top of the plant down onto the immature cobs that form about halfway up the stem. To increase the chances of pollination the plants should be planted in groups in a block formation rather than singly or in rows. If you want to grow sweetcorn in a pot or container, make sure it is of considerable size and weight as, being so tall, the plants could be at risk of being blown over in a strong wind. For containers, the spacing should ideally not be less than 30cm (1ft) apart and growing in a raised bed or outside vegetable patch, 45cm (18") minimum. The soil depth should be a minimum of 30cm to give the plant plenty of room to anchor itself.

Seed needs to be sown in April into deep modules (root trainers are the best) or into peat pots because sweetcorn dislikes having its roots disturbed when transplanted. Outside, you can sow direct in May. Germination usually takes around 10-12 days. Harden the young plants off before transplanting outdoors. The plants will grow rapidly and will need frequent watering thoughout the summer, allowing the cobs to swell. In August or September, depending on the variety you are growing, the sweetcorn will be ready to harvest! Once the 'silks' at the top of each cob have turned brown, test each one for ripeness by gently pulling back a protective leaf covering the cob. Dig your thumbnail into one of the grains: if a creamy coloured liquid squirts out the sweetcorn is ripe. If left too late, the liquid will be thicker and sticky and the cob will be too tough, so it pays to check your crop regularly (every couple of days). Remove the ripe cobs off the stem with a twisting action – just before running back to the kitchen with them!

Varieties of sweetcorn:
There are four different classifications for sweetcorn varieties, but I would urge you not to get bogged down

too much with the complexities or the advantages of one over another, at least when you are growing sweetcorn for the first time. Just so you know what they are I am listing the classifications here so that they will at least be familiar to you if you come across them on a seed packet. The categories are: Normal sugar type; Sugar enhanced; Super sweet; Extra tender. Normal sugar is the standard sweetcorn.

Some varieties (All F1): Normal Sugar: Earligold, Sundance. Sugar enhanced: Miracle, Incredible. Super sweet: Earlibird , Ovation. Extra tender: Swift, Lark.

Florence Fennel

An unusual vegetable that is gaining in popularity and just looks so amazing when it is growing. The large white edible bulb is topped with glorious green feathery leaves that can also be eaten chopped up in salads to give a crisp, aniseed flavour. The trick is to keep the plants warm and moist all through the growing season – a lack of water can make the plants run to seed prematurely before the bulbs are fully grown. I have always raised my plants in module trays; the young plants look delicate but transplant well. The best time to sow is April onwards, depending on the variety. The best place to plant them out is a warm and sheltered position in the garden or to put several in a container (15cm apart minimum). They can also be grown singly in litre (13cm) pots. Mulching the surface will significantly help retain water and a liquid feed now and again will be very beneficial to growth. Pick when the bulbs are nice and fat.

Aubergines

A prolonged, hot summer is needed for aubergines to

Flowerpot Farming

fruit successfully outdoors. The best place to grow them, apart from a greenhouse or polytunnel, is in a warm conservatory or on a windowsill and the best way to start them off is by sowing the seeds in small pots, 2 to a pot, indoors, on a light, warm windowsill. Germination will take 2 to 3 weeks. When the young plants are large enough they can be planted up individually into 9 inch pots or into a grow bag which will accommodate 3 per bag.

Once the plants are about 30cm (12") high, pinch out the top, which will encourage side shoots to develop and the fruit will form on these. Aubergines like high humidity and a daily mist with water using a small plant spray or a container filled with water will help keep the air around the plants moist. Feed weekly with a tomato fertiliser as soon as you can see tiny fruits developing. Once 5 or so fruits have started to form, remove any others to ensure the remaining ones reach a good size. Generally the fruits are ready for picking once they reach a decent size and have a glossy shine to them.

Herbs

One of the purposes of this book is to convince you that growing your own fruit and vegetables can be a reality wherever you live; that most are ideal for container and small space growing, but herbs are simply perfect for any window box, container, raised bed, pot or in fact anywhere you care to plant them. By the kitchen window or back door is probably the most convenient place so they are readily to hand when you are cooking – if you are anything like me, herbs are a case of 'out of sight, out of mind', but if they are close to the kitchen, hopefully that won't be the case!

Space precludes me from explaining every single herb,

cultivation method and culinary use for each (although I would love to!), but the following list includes many of the most useful and popular – and all are suitable for both containers and growing direct in the garden. I have split them down into annuals (and biennials) and perennials which I hope will help you when planning your planting schemes. There are several excellent books dedicated entirely to herbs, some of which are listed in the 'further reading' section.

Annuals: parsley (curly, French, and Giant Italian, the latter two both flat leaf, and is actually a biennial because it can survive over winter then go to seed the following year, but it is normally treated as an annual), basil (all varieties), coriander, chervil and dill.

Perennials: mint, marjoram, oregano, rosemary, sage, lovage, fennel, chives, bay, thyme, tarragon (a tender perennial which will need to be given some protection for it to survive through the winter). Bay and rosemary can grow into very large, impressive specimens and could eventually be given a whole container to themselves.

Chapter Five
Planting Ideas

An orchard on your patio

Even if you haven't a lot of space to spare you really can have a mini orchard. Fruit trees and bushes don't have to be large specimens - there are many varieties that have dwarf forms which you can grow in containers. Apples and other tree fruits such as cherries on dwarfing rootstocks are ideal for growing on a patio or in a courtyard in large pots. If you have a bit more space, and the soil to grow them in, you could choose to grow an espalier which can be trained to grow against a wall. There are small, vertical apple trees called 'ballerinas' which can be squeezed into a fairly limited space. A fairly recent introduction and worth looking out for are 'family' trees, which have several different varieties of apple grafted onto one rootstock. Pollination issues and limited choice of fruit need not worry you any more! Unfortunately pears are not available on the smaller rootstocks and are threrefore too vigorous unless you are growing them in open ground. However, orange and lemon trees do particularly well grown in pots and containers and they are small enough to be moved indoors when required in winter.

A fig can be grown successfully in a pot too, but likes a sunny position and you'll need to protect it well over the winter – either by bringing it inside somewhere cool and frost free or by using straw, bubble wrap, sacking or fleece to insulate it during the coldest months of winter. The most common variety you will see is 'Brown Turkey', a tried and tested fig.

Bush fruits such as blueberries, cranberries and gooseberries are other good candidates for container growing and they take up less space than tree fruit. They can, if left unattended, end up as large bushes, but if pruned lightly each year to keep their shape it is possible to have both berries and a neat looking fruit bush.

With all fruit in pots, just make sure you plant them in good quality compost rich in organic matter. This will give the fruit trees a lot of nutrients and a moisture retaining medium in which to grow. Even though you shouldn't allow your fruit trees to dry out, make sure they are not drowning in water either by placing a thick layer of gravel at the bottom of the pots before adding the compost.

Although it cannot remotely be described as an orchard fruit, a grapevine will grow in a large container and, because it can be trained over walls, up trellises and along a vertical or horizontal area, it is easy to fit into a fruit garden theme. Grapes like to be planted deeply without any restriction to their roots so the bigger the container the better. Make sure they are treated to lots of well-rotted manure or compost when planting. A sheltered spot in the sun will be ideal for your grapevine. Given a good summer, you will be able to harvest grapes after 2 or 3 years. Always choose outdoor varieties and you will be more assured of success. I grew the well-known traditional 'Black Hamburg' in a big pot trained up the outside of a conservatory for several years and it grew extremely well. In fact, I still have it – but it is now planted into the soil and climbs and over a pergola in my garden!

All fruit grown in pots will be vulnerable to the cold throughout the winter. Even with the hardiest of apples, if they are grown in containers it is important to keep the roots well insulated while the weather is at its coldest. Wrapping the pots in insulating material such as bubble wrap, straw and sacking will keep the cold away from the roots.

Choosing your varieties

As regards the most appropriate varieties, your choice will be dictated by what is available on either an M9 or M27 rootstock. Please refer to p.66/p.67 (Apples) for more information on this subject

Selecting your pots and containers

Terracotta certainly looks the part when it has a tree or fruit bush growing in it. Clay is also heavier than plastic so less likely to fall over in the wind. As the material is porous it does mean you will have to water them more frequently, but they are good for the plants because they are cooler in summer and warmer in the winter.

A runner bean arbour

You will need: 1 ready made garden arch made from plastic coated metal, a wooden arch or thin trellis panels. A small seat or simple bench. Six runner bean plants. String to tie them against the structure as they grow. Containers for each plant or pair of plants.

Vegetables can be both productive and beautiful, and none more so than when grown over a covered seat. Runner beans have wonderful large green leaves so are ideal for shading a secluded seat and, during the summer, are covered in pretty red, white or red/white flowers, depending on the variety grown. You could just as easily choose to grow climbing beans in the same way, but runners tend to look just that little bit fuller and lusher. And, because they are only annuals, your arbour can be temporary if you wish and can be moved into other positions in your garden from one year to the next.

Planting can be done directly into the soil if the structure is sited in your garden, or the beans can be sown in containers evenly positioned around the base of the arbour. If you prefer you can raise the plants from seed in small pots and then transplant the plants into their final positions when they are about 15cm tall. Beans need well drained, fertile soil and have relatively shallow roots for such tall plants, but allow them the largest containers you realistically can – the more soil around their roots, the more water will be retained. Runner and climbing beans will need a generous supply of water all through their growing season; not surprising for such vigorous, fast growing plants that geminate, grow several feet, flower and then give enormous crops in the space of just 4-5 months!

Flowerpot Farming

Varieties: there are several to choose from and most garden centres will offer a good choice. A runner bean with completely red flowers is 'Scarlet Emperor', red and white flowers are found on 'Painted Lady', white flowers on 'White Emergo' and salmon pink on 'Celebration'. (For more detailed cultivation instructions, see Chapter 4).

Siting the arbour

The arch frame will need to be secured firmly, fixed to a wall or, if free-standing, held in place by burying at least 24cm (8") into the soil and then attached to stakes in the ground for extra stability. Runner beans can grow to over 10 feet if given the chance so will easily cover the arch. They will also be surprisingly heavy, especially when the beans are maturing, and you won't want to take the risk of them being blown over in a high wind.

If your arbour is situated on open soil then all you need to do is sow the seeds evenly around the frame. The beans need to be spaced about 24cm (8") apart, but sow two seeds into each position to allow for any failures (you can always remove the weaker one if both seeds germinate). If you are growing the beans completely in individual pots then you can put them somewhere sheltered and move them into position once the plants are large enough. Your beans will soon start to grow vigorously and will need to be tied onto the frame at regular intervals as they grow. The last (and nicest) task of all is to move a comfortable seat into the middle of the arbour and think of all the tasty beans you will be eating in a few months' time!

A window box with a Mediterranean feel

You will need: 1 window box or trough to fit beneath your window sill. Fixings to hold the box securely in place. 1 plastic sheet to line the box if wooden. 2 tomato plants ('Totem' – dwarf variety). 6 sweet or bush basil plants. 3 dwarf pepper plants (1 x F1 'Apache', 1x 'Bulgarian Carrot', 1 x 'Mohawk'. 6 oregano herbs.

The secret to successful growing in small spaces is using the best quality compost you can find and feeding the growing plants with regular doses of organic feed through the summer. This will make sure you get a continuous crop over a long period. For a 'themed' window box like this one, you might want to choose something brightly coloured to reflect the nature of the plants that will grow in it, or choose a more natural looking box such as wood, and let the plants speak for themselves. You might instead want to tie it in with the outside design of your house, or for a more personal touch get your children to paint it in vivid colours. Whatever you decide on, the bigger the capacity the window box has, the better for your plants and remember that drainage is vital, so holes in the bottom are a must.

Plant the trough up with the tomatoes and peppers spaced out along the back, with the small herbs situated at the front. An alternative could be to plant a variety of creeping thyme or rosemary at the front, which in time will scramble attractively over the edge of the trough. They will smell good too!

Window boxes full of compost, plants and water are extremely heavy, so make sure the wall fixings are adequate for the maximum weight and size of box you are using and that the wall or window frame you are

Flowerpot Farming

attaching it to is able to take the weight. If it is a load bearing outside wall you could increase the security of your window box by fixing up an additional frame, ideally made of steel or wood and held in place with heavy duty masonry fittings.

Come summer you will have a taste of the Mediterranean just outside your window; tomatoes, peppers and the herbs to complement them.

Hanging baskets of plenty

If you normally have a floral display of flowers in hanging baskets outside your house, why not do something a little different this year and use them to grow vegetables or herbs instead? They can look just as attractive and be productive at the same time.

Great candidates for hanging baskets are trailing, dwarf varieties of tomato (particularly recommended is the variety 'Tumbler' with tiny, sweet fruits formed on plants with leaves that will eventually cover the baskets they are held in), strawberries and trailing herbs (look out especially for creeping rosemary, creeping lemon/red thyme and pennyroyal (spreading with lilac flowers and a minty flavour) as they all do well in baskets.

Vegetables in baskets are best sited in a sheltered position and, in common with all basket plants, should never be allowed to dry out completely. Make sure your plants are fed regularly – this applies particularly to the fruiting vegetables as the crop will be severely checked if subjected to a lack of water.

Any of the preformed basket liners are suitable for lining your basket before putting in the compost. Moss is a traditional liner but try and find out, if you can, just

128

where it has come from. Some mosses are taken from the wild, stripping the area they come from of a valuable resource. Moss that is grown especially for use as a liner is a far better environmental choice (or if you do have a moss-infested lawn like mine, you could use some of that!).

A raised bed on a patio or in the garden

A great way to enable you to grow some of the vegetables that require deeper soil than most containers can hold is to use a raised bed. Not only will you be able to grow root vegetables such as carrots, beetroot and parsnips, but a raised bed will bring whatever you grow in it up to a more convenient height for routine plant maintenance and picking. If you have back problems then growing vegetables in this way will become a pleasure as the higher the bed, the less you will have to bend.

You can either construct your raised bed yourself from scratch using timber, or buy one of the kits that are widely available from gardening suppliers. These will come ready to assemble. Other than a traditional wooden raised bed, a more permanent structure could be made from bricks in the form of a low wall built to enclose either a rectangle or a square. This would look best in a formal setting such as a courtyard or on a large patio.

The raised bed I am describing here is very simple to make, will only take a couple of hours and you don't have to be a DIY expert. The rustic look of the bed should fit in with many different settings. The materials are not expensive, and you can always use secondhand wood to bring the costs down further.

Constructing the raised bed

Decide where the bed is going and use a line to mark it out. It is better to make a narrow bed where you can reach the middle from both sides, than one in which you have to step on the soil to get to all your plants. After clearing away all perennial weeds, ensure that the site is

level and check the diagonals to see that the bed is square.

Having marked out and checked that you are happy with the layout, you will now be able to work out what you need in the way of wood for the sides. A good choice is secondhand scaffolding planks if they are in reasonably good condition. Don't use wood that is too thin, like floorboards, because they will quickly rot. Four internal corner posts will also be needed to hold the whole structure together – 3" x 3" square fencing posts are ideal for this.

The posts should be driven into the ground at least 18"
and cut off level with the top edge of the boards. Fix the
boards to the posts using non-rusting screws.

Stair finial balls fixed onto each of the corners is a nice
finishing touch, but is also useful too because they can
stop your hosepipe dragging across the plants.
Fill the bed evenly with good quality top soil mixed
with compost or well rotted manure to within an inch
or 25mm below the top of the boards. Leave it to settle
and top up as required. Your raised deep bed is now
ready to plant.

Patio Potatoes

You don't need acres of space to grow your own tasty
new potatoes or even a spare patch of ground in your
garden because you can grow your own tasty potatoes in
containers on your balcony or patio! Growing potatoes
in containers also means that you don't have to hunt

around for the tubers in the soil either because you can simply tip the whole plant out and, hey presto! the potatoes are all ready to be harvested.

If you want the very easiest option, a number of seed companies now offer potato patio kits. These consist of sturdy woven polyethelene sacks with drainage holes and carrying handles so they can be moved around if required. The seed potatoes are included so all you need to do is supply the compost.

An alternative is a potato barrel or planter. The tubers grown inside it can be easily 'earthed up' to encourage large crops. Some designs incorporate a sliding outer sleeve at the base of the planter so the potatoes can be harvested without having to dig up the plants.

It's also very easy to grow potatoes in your own containers. A large bucket or pot can be half filled with compost and the chitted tubers planted in it and, as the shoots grow, you simply add more layers to fill the bucket. When the potatoes are ready the bucket is tipped up and the potatoes are easily harvested. A similar method using old tyres or bottomless stacking trays can be used adding another tyre or tray and filling it with compost as the plants grow. Perhaps not the most attractive proposition for your patio, but it works for Bob Flowerdew!

Chapter Six
Further Steps for the Flowerpot Farmer

Once your urban farm has been up and running for a year or so, you might want to take on a little more. It could be something simple like saving some seed from your own vegetables or making your own liquid fertilisers and feeds to save you having to buy them in. Or it could be the much bigger step of taking on an allotment. There's always something new to learn about vegetable gardening which adds to its interest – there are always new growing techniques to try, newly introduced varieties to grow, and changing weather patterns year by year to keep us on our toes.

One of the great things about gardening is that there's always something new to learn and the more you speak to other gardeners, the more ideas you'll pick up. The art

Flowerpot Farming

of vegetable growing is definitely not an exact science and the beauty of it for me is that you can sometimes bend the rules a little and still get good results. And if something does fail you can always try again next year. With quick growing vegetables you can often even start again straight away.

Another way of learning more about vegetable growing is to visit places such as the excellent headquarters of Garden Organic in Ryton-on-Dunsmore near Coventry. I first went there in the early 1980s and saw it in its fledgling state just a year after it was opened and have tried to visit regularly ever since. In the intervening years the gardens have developed and are a real inspiration to organic gardeners everywhere as well as a great source of ideas for getting the best use out of small spaces. A major feature of the gardens is that much of the site is divided into many urban sized gardens, in which vegetables feature heavily. The size and scale of these gardens reflects the sizes of ordinary town gardens, and each one has a slightly different slant in what it contains. As well as the model gardens there is also a fantastic shop offering everything from gardening tools and requisites, books, gifts and an organic food shop. The excellent Heritage Seed Library is also run by Garden Organic and I would recommend joining it if you want to try growing old and unusual vegetable seed that you can't buy anywhere else. The library offers seed to its members which have been deleted from the 'seed list' and so are illegal to sell elsewhere, but by joining you are entitled to 6 different varieties of seed per year. Much of the seed is made available through other members, volunteers called 'seed guardians' who grow the parent plants through to maturity, collect the seed and forward it back to the seed library for other members. If such names as 'Carruther's Purple Podded' bean, Whippersnapper' pea, 'Mr Stiff's Bunching Onion'

134

and broad bean 'Bonnie Lad' grab your imagination then maybe you should join the HSA too.

The Victorians knew a thing or two about vegetable gardening, particularly the skilful gardeners employed in the large country houses of the day. The growing methods followed were mostly along organic lines (but not all – think nicotine sprays!), and they maximised the space in enclosed walled gardens. Tender fruit trees were trained up walls and many different types of vegetable were crammed in to provide the master of the manor with a wide array of produce for his dining table. Many of these grand walled gardens have fallen into disuse, but some have thankfully been restored and are open to the public. A couple worth mentioning are the walled gardens at Audley End House in Essex and Normanby Hall in North Lincolnshire – a day spent wandering around one of these or many other similar restoration projects would be worthwhile and will definitely give you some inspiration.

Should you feel the need to widen your knowledge still further, then apart from reading a few of the excellent books available at the moment, some of which are listed in the back section of this book, you could enrol on a gardening course. Not all are geared solely for vegetable growers, however, and are perhaps more attractive to people interested in all aspects of gardening. However, two well recognised qualifications to aim for are the RHS General and the City & Guilds Gardening certificate, both of which focus sections of the course on fruit and vegetables and are good if you want to come away with a certificate to prove your knowledge. Nearer to home you might be lucky and come across a gardening evening class at a local education centre.

A more 'hands on' step is to have a go at making your

own liquid feeds and I'd recommend you try this quite early on in your vegetable growing because the plants will love them and you'll get great results. They are an excellent source of nourishment for all your garden plants and especially good for your vegetable crops. Liquid fertiliser provides extra goodness which is extracted when leaves and stalks ferment in water. Plants treated to regular doses of liquid feed build increased resistance to disease. These recipes are completely organic too and everyone should be able to get hold of the ingredients for the first one... stinging nettle liquid!

Stinging Nettle Liquid

Ingredients: one plastic bucket or similar container, half a bucketful of young nettle leaves and stems and one bucketful of water.

If you haven't got a garden then you should be able to find some nettles in neglected spaces in local parks, friends' gardens(!) or wasteland. I don't recommend collecting them from verges alongside busy roads because of possible pollution from the passing traffic.

Fill your chosen container halfway with nettles, then top it up to the brim with water. Cover with wire netting to keep the plants under the water. Air needs to be incorporated to aid the decomposition process, so give the mixture a stir every day. Soon the liquid will start to smell and will become darker – the fermentation process has started! Leave it for a week or two (depending on the temperature) and it is ready to be diluted for use.

It is said that the potent smell of nettle liquid can be minimised by adding a handful of bonemeal or pungent herbs such as rosemary or thyme. I've always tried to keep mine away from the house in the hope that no one will notice the smell!

Nettle liquid is very concentrated and always needs diluting before putting on your plants. It contains large amounts of potash and nitrogen. Dilution should be no less than 1:5 nettles to water and more usually 1:10. You can use a watering can or spray to feed it to your plants.

Comfrey Liquid Feed

This is used and made in exactly the same way as nettle liquid. Comfrey is a hardy perennial plant rich in potash with useful levels of nitrogen and phosphate. It thrives in light shade and is easy to grow if you want it for supplying you with ingredients for a liquid feed. The best one to grow for this purpose is 'Bocking 14', a variety of Russian comfrey. The leaves can also be harvested and placed around plants like tomatoes and soft fruit as a nutrient rich mulch. As a liquid feed comfrey concentrate needs to be diluted between 1:10 and 1:20.

Animal Manure Liquid Feed

For this potent 'recipe' you can use horse, sheep or cow manure. You will need a large plastic bucket or water butt, several handfuls of manure from your chosen animal, a ladies stocking or one leg of a pair of tights and water.

Fill the bucket or butt with water. Stuff the animal manure down into the foot section of the stocking or tights, then suspend this into the water butt, tying the top of the stocking around a cane or stick which can then be rested on the rim of the container so the manure is completely submerged in the water. Leave for 2-3 weeks, occasionally swirling the manure around every few days or so. The liquid manure is now ready to use, but will need diluting 2:1 before watering in around your plants. Feeding with the mixture can be done weekly in the growing/fruiting season.

Making your own compost

However small your plot, you should try to have a go at making your own compost from the waste from your kitchen and garden. It is easy to do and costs almost nothing once you have set up the system you are going to use. A small garden should be able to sustain at least one compost bin; if you only have a balcony or small outside space you can still put your kitchen waste to good use by setting up a 'wormery'.

The compost bin

Using a compost bin will turn your kitchen and garden waste into valuable organic matter that you can use to enrich your soil by digging it in or using it as a mulch around your plants. You are aiming for an end product which is sweet-smelling and a rich deep brown colour with a crumbly texture. Adding compost to your soil will improve its structure and provide food for your vegetable plants.

Choose a compost bin that suits your garden; small enough to fit into a small space but large enough to produce worthwhile amounts of lovely organic compost. Most garden centres and gardening sections of DIY shops will have at least one or two to choose from. You are most likely to come across the traditional sectional square wooden bins. These can take up quite a lot of space but their natural appearance means they can be

easily disguised in a corner or even hidden by using them for scrambling vegetable plants. Because they are built up in sections, it means you can partially dismantle them for the purpose of getting a fork in and performing the essential task of turning over the contents and incorporating oxygen which allows the materials to break down quicker.

Plastic compost bins are reasonably cheap to purchase and some councils provide a compost bin for free so it's certainly worth contacting your local council to see if they run this initiative.

Some bins are fixed onto stands so that they can be flipped over completely in order to turn the contents and incorporate air. Turning the bin over every three days or so will mean your compost will be ready for use in just a few weeks. Static plastic bins are more awkward to use because of the confined area for getting into the bins to turn the compost, but of course won't rot. Look out for bins with a height of not more than a metre which will save your back when forking over the contents.

Practically all garden waste can be added to your compost bin, although perennial weeds, plant matter that is diseased and meat or cooked kitchen scraps should definitely not be added. Try to get a mixture of green waste such as grass clippings, annual weeds, old vegetable plants, fruit and veg peelings that are rich in nitrogen and carbon rich ingredients like plant stems, shredded newspaper and/or cardboard and woody prunings (thick ones should be shredded or chopped small to aid decomposition). A mixture of these two distinct types of waste will allow air to circulate. Green waste only will result in a slimy smelly mess – coarser carbon rich ingredients aerate the heap. Turning the heap at monthly intervals will add more oxygen. Keep the top of the bin covered at all times to keep the heat in and the rain out. The heat generated will decompose the contents, turning it into lovely rich compost in the space of a few months. Do make sure that rainwater does not wash away these precious nutrients into the soil around your bin!

A wormery

If you haven't got the space for a compost bin, and won't have much in the way of plant material to add to it, you can still produce worthwhile amounts of high quality, nutritious compost using a worm bin. With it you will be able to recycle your own kitchen waste, turning it into food for your plants. You can make your own wormery or buy one ready made. Worm bins aren't smelly, they don't take up very much room and you will be doing a little bit more for the environment by recycling your kitchen scraps and creating food for the vegetables you are growing. Even if you have a compost heap on the go, why not have a wormery too? Because it is kept in a frost free place through the winter, a worm bin will continue to produce a little compost all year round, whilst an outside bin may not be doing a lot in the colder months. The best time of year to start your wormery is once the temperature starts to warm up in late spring and early summer. This will encourage your worms to establish themselves quickly in their new home and start feeding and breeding.

Buying a ready made wormery

Purpose made worm bins can be bought from DIY shops, garden centres and through mail order. Some of these come complete with worms (or more usually a voucher to get your worms once your system is up and ready to go) and instructions on how to get started. One of the best systems is made up of round plastic trays which fit, one on top of the other. The bottom tray is fitted with a tap which allows any liquid accumulated at the bottom to be drained off and used as a liquid feed. The worms start off in the bottom chamber, eating their way up as the 'food' is added. The process will take several months until you have a worthwhile amount of useable compost, but what you will get is very high quality, beautiful, crumbly and rich and better than compost made in the normal way in an outside compost bin. Because the quantities produced are fairly small it is perfect for using for container gardening and can be used to top dress around your vegetables or very lightly dug in before planting.

Making your own worm bin

Ready made wormeries are initially quite expensive to buy and so you might want to have a go at making one yourself to save some money. You don't need to buy a lot of equipment; a simple plastic household dustbin can be easily converted. If you are going to use a plastic bin then choose one that is not too tall and make sure that it has a lid.

The bin will need to have a couple of rows of drainage holes all around the bottom to allow excess moisture to drain out and another set around the top to allow air into the bin when the lid is on. The lower set of holes should be positioned about 3cm from the base and made with a drill at regular intervals all around the diameter of the bin. The holes towards the top should be made in the same way.

Start by filling the bin with a layer of gravel which should be sufficient to go just over the level of the lower drainage holes. Then place some pieces of thin wood on top to stop the upper contents getting mixed in with the gravel. This wood should not be packed too tightly together to allow for drainage. After that you will need to add a layer of material for the worms to initially live in before they begin to start moving up through the upper layer and start making compost. Ideal material for this is shredded up damp newspaper and/or cardboard, leaf mould or well matured compost.

Now you are ready to introduce the worms! As you have probably guessed, these aren't just the ordinary worms you can find in the garden. The best type for our purpose is known as the brandling or tiger worm. These can be bought via mail order through the same suppliers that sell the complete wormery kits or through fishing tackle shops as they are frequently used as bait by anglers. The worms are sold by the gram, and of course the more you have, the quicker things will get moving. 500gms should be plenty to start with – that's roughly 1000 individuals!

Empty your worms onto the layer of bedding you have provided and lightly cover them with a layer of chopped kitchen waste. Don't bury them completely. Leave a few gaps and cover over the whole surface with a thick layer of cardboard. It may take several weeks for the worms to acclimatize and to start eating the waste, but once they do add a little more. Try not to overfeed them because the food will start to decay before the worms manage to eat it and the bin will then start to smell nasty. In the summer your worms will be able to work through more waste than in the winter when the temperature falls, so cut their food down accordingly. If you are using a plastic dustbin, place the lid on top to keep the moisture in and the light out.

You could just as easily adapt or make up a wooden box to house your composting worms. One with a slatted base would be ideal, or you could drill holes to let the excess moisture out. The layers should be made up in exactly the same way as the instructions given for the plastic bin, the only difference being that you need to keep the surface from drying out by topping it with damp newspaper and loosely covering the top of the box with black polythene.

Flowerpot Farming

A wormery is the ideal soluction for the urban kitchen garden. Photo Wiggly Wigglers.

What you can feed your worms on...

Vegetable and fruit peelings (but not citrus fruit), egg shells, tea leaves/coffee grounds, cooked vegetables, annual weeds and fresh waste from your veg crops, shredded paper and stale bread.

But definitely not meat, fish, grass cuttings, perennial weeds, plants carrying disease and dairy foods.

Where to keep your worm bin

Ideally worms need cool and moist conditions to work effectively; in fact to breathe. The material you add to it should keep it fairly moist, but it's best to check now and again to make sure the drainage system is working and that the worms aren't getting waterlogged or, at the other end of the scale, too dry. Site your worm bin somewhere out of the direct sun in the warmer months and keep it frost free in winter by moving it somewhere protected. You could insulate it with bubble wrap or an old blanket or carpet, but whatever you do, make sure the contents are kept from freezing, or the worms will die.

Collecting your compost

The day will come when your worm compost is ready.

Normally this will take a few months but exactly how many depends on the outside temperature and how many worms are breaking down the materials you are feeding them. You can harvest some of the compost a little at a time or wait a bit longer for a larger quantity to become ready. Just as spring and summer is a good time for starting off a new wormery, the same time of year is best for harvesting your compost. Then the worms will have plenty of time to replenish their compost layer to live in over the winter.

First of all you will need to remove the top layer of waste, any partially digested waste and most of the worms themselves, which should be close to the surface. This should be put to one side and put back once you have removed the compost you need. The rest of the compost will still have some worms in it. If you are using the compost in containers, then you will probably want to remove as many of the remaining worms as you can, but if the compost is being used straight on the garden the worms could be left in it. To separate the remaining worms from the compost you want to use, spread the compost out on a solid surface – it helps if it is a bright sunny day – and cover one side of it with damp sheets of newspaper or cardboard. Leave it for a couple of hours then return. You will find that most of the worms have retreated under the damp paper. These can then be returned to the bin with the others to start the process off once again.

The crumbly, earthy, sweet smelling compost you are left with can be used in all sorts of beneficial ways on your vegetables. As I have already said, it can be put to good use as a top dressing in your containers. Fruit trees in pots will benefit greatly from the nutrient boost. Pop some of it into planting holes when you are transplanting your vegetables into their final pots so it reaches the roots: hungry, fast growing crops such as tomatoes, cucumbers and squashes need all the nutrients they can get. But really, worm compost is great for using anywhere and the beauty of it is that it has all been made from scraps and waste normally destined for the dustbin.

Saving seed

It might be that you will be eating all the vegetables you produce before they have a chance to set seed. In fact, in a limited growing space this will probably very likely be the case, but if you want to go full-circle and produce the seed for next year's crops then it's possible and very satisfying to do so. If you like a particular variety of vegetable and are planning to buy more seed to grow it again the following year, then why not save some seed from your old crop. It won't cost you anything for the seed and you will be following the old-fashioned way of growing vegetables. If you belong to a seed library such as the Heritage Seed Library run by Garden Organic, you will need to save seed anyway for the following year if you want to grow that vegetable again. If you have plenty of saved seed to spare, you could even send some back to them or run a seed swap with another gardener. Whatever your own reasons for wanting to save seed from your own crops, by doing so you may never have to buy another seed again – and that really is self-sufficiency!

One point to bear in mind is the type of vegetable seeds you bought from the seed supplier in the first place. Modern 'F1' varieties of vegetable seed have been bred and hybridized to produce high yielding, disease resistant strains of vegetables. The crops they produce at the end of the growing season are uniform and usually very reliable – a big plus point to all the farmers and growers who rely on good yields year on year, and who cannot afford to see a crop fail or produce an inferior yield because of disease or other outside influences. This comes at a price – these hybrids will not 'breed true', that is, you will not end up with an exact replica of the same vegetable the following year from seed produced by its parent. This is not a problem for the commercial grower who will buy in new seed from the merchant the following year, and not a problem for the majority of gardeners who also buy in fresh seed each season.

The older 'open pollinated' varieties are the ones to choose if you are thinking about saving seed, because the seed you save from these has not been tampered with and the seed you collect will produce a replica of its parent, provided it has not cross pollinated with another variety of the same vegetable! Some vegetable families cross pollinate readily with each other if they are grown within a certain distance of each other (thanks to bees and similar flying insects, which are invaluable for the pollination and formation of our crops in the first place). A good example is the brassica (cabbage) family (including cabbages, broccoli, calabrese, cauliflower, etc.), each different variety of which would need to be grown at least 500 metres apart to prevent this! No backyard vegetable plots have the luxury of being able to grow their varieties this far apart, but all is not lost because there are ways to get round this problem. For collecting small amounts of seed you could cover individual flower heads with a small paper bag to avoid cross pollination with other plants. However you will need to pollinate the flowers yourself by gently brushing across the surface of the flowers with a small paintbrush. This will ensure fertilization and seed formation.

Some other vegetables, such as tomatoes and French beans, are self-pollinating and so the chances of cross

Flowerpot Farming

pollination are very low indeed.

You will be able to tell from the seed packets and the seed catalogues which varieties are hybrids because they will include 'F1' in their titles. For example, both cucumbers 'Marketmore' and 'Telegraph' are older varieties still widely available, but are becoming outnumbered amongst the more numerous modern types such as 'Flamingo F1' and 'Klaro F1'. The improvements of the hybrid cucumbers include the plants only producing female flowers which makes life for the gardener slightly easier as he/she doesn't have to pick off the male flowers which give the fruits a bitter flavour if allowed to pollinate naturally.

Collecting seed from your plants is quite easy, and of course some varieties of vegetables are easier than others to harvest seed from. Always choose the healthiest and best specimen plants from which to take your seeds. Runner and climbing beans are really easy to do. All you need is to resist picking a few of the pods later in the season, then wait for them to dry out and turn brown on the plant. This really is best done once the plant has almost finished cropping or you have had plenty of them to eat, because with beans, if you leave any beans on the plant to mature, it will inhibit flower production and therefore stop producing beans. Pick off the dry pods on a dry day and store the seeds in a paper bag, either still in the pod or shelled. The seeds should be nice and firm. Fruiting vegetables are slightly more tricky but it is still a reasonably simple matter to save the seed. Take tomatoes, for example. Wait until the tomatoes are really ripe (you can store them indoors) and soft to the touch, then split them open and scoop out all the seed onto a piece of kitchen paper. This will absorb most of the moisture. Transfer them onto a clean piece of kitchen paper and leave them to dry naturally.

Once they are completely dry, the seeds can be stored away.

Always make sure the seed is completely dry before you store it somewhere safe for next year, and store them in small paper bags (not polythene) or envelopes. There's nothing worse than opening the seed container when you are all ready to sow the following spring to find that the seed has gone mouldy. Don't forget to write the details of the vegetable and variety on the outside of the bag or envelope. Store your packets of seed in an airtight tin and keep it in a cool room or, if you have room in your fridge, in an airtight jar. Most seed will keep an average of 2-3 years if it is stored properly, although some seed, such as parsnip, will only keep for a year (see Appendices for details specific to each vegetable).

Buying a greenhouse

Once you start getting serious about producing your own food, and have some outside space available, you might want to consider buying a greenhouse. This will bring with it lots of advantages and will take your vegetable growing into a new dimension.

Imagine having lots of space just for propagating your plants from seed and somewhere to pot up vegetables, as well as an area where you can grow more delicate vegetables such as indoor tomatoes, cucumbers and melons. And you can carry on gardening in comfort even if the rain is pouring down outdoors. If you have a little outside space you will certainly be able to find room for a small but perfectly formed greenhouse. It doesn't have to be sited on soil, it can just as easily be fitted onto your patio if you have one, and the plants can be grown in grow bags or pots on the floor. There are even lean-to styles that can be attached to the outer

Flowerpot Farming

walls of your house.

Greenhouses don't have to be big – you can still fit a worthwhile amount of plants into a modestly sized one. As there is a huge choice of manufacturers you are bound to find exactly the model you want from the sizes, materials and designs available. You can choose from frames made of aluminum or wood, glazing of polycarbonate or traditional horticultural glass. Cost is usually a limiting factor when choosing a greenhouse, but aim to get the largest one you can afford (that will still fit into your available space!) because, however big it is, once you start filling it with vegetables it is never quite large enough. A good choice for an urban garden is a 6ft x 8ft aluminium traditional greenhouse glazed with horticultural glass from roof to floor. This allows the maximum amount of light to reach the plants inside and provides enough space to put a couple of lengths of staging along one side for seed trays and young seedlings, leaving the other side free to grow tall plants such as cucumbers and tomatoes. Two opening windows (one with a vent which opens automatically) plus a sliding door at one end will provide adequate ventilation.

On a smaller scale, a budget 'greenhouse' that takes the form of a simple, tiered frame with a polythene cover is useful if you are running out of room on your windowsills. These can be purchased very cheaply from gardening sections in most DIY stores, but they do work. If sited in a sunny position the warmth really will get your seeds off to a flying start in spring. It can be used for both germinating seeds and growing on young plants prior to planting into their final containers or final positions out in the garden.

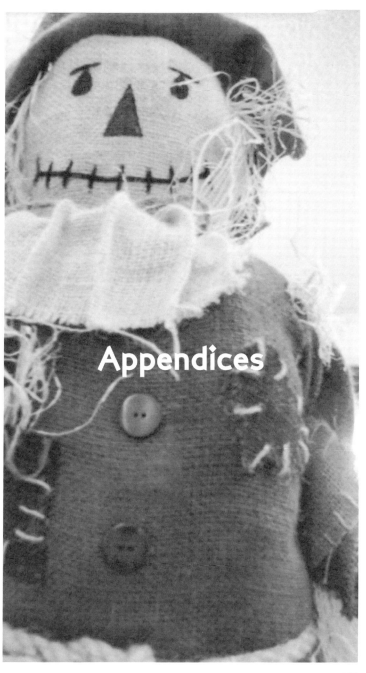

Appendices

Further Reading
Grow Your Own Vegetables by Joy Larkcom.
The Vegetable Expert by Dr. D. G. Hessayon
The Fruit Expert by Dr. D. G. Hessayon
New Book of Herbs by Jekka McVicar
The Fruit Book by Bob Flowerdew
Organic Gardening By Lawrence D. Hills
Encylopedia of Organic Gardening Ed. Pauline Pears
All About Compost by Pauline Pears and Charlotte Green.
Vegetables in a Small Garden: an RHS publication
TheWindow-Box Allotment by Penelope Bennett.

Specialist Suppliers
Deacons Nursery, Moor View, Godshill, Isle of Wight PO38 3HW. 01983 840750 www.deaconsnurseryfruits.co.uk.

Dobies of Devon, Long Road, Paignton, Devon TQ4 7SX. 0844 7017625 www.dobies.co.uk.

D. T. Brown, Bury Road, Newmarket, Suffolk CB8 7PQ. 0845 1662275 www.dtbrownseeds.co.uk.

Seeds of Italy (Franchi), C3 Phoenix Industrial Estate, Rosslyn Crescent, Harrow HA1 22SP. 0208 427 5020 www.seedsofita-ly.com.

Plants of Distinction, Abacus House, Station Yard, Needham Market, Suffolk IP6 8AS. 01449 721722 www.plantsofdistinc-tion.co.uk.

Kings Seeds, Monks Farm, Kelvedon, Colchester, Essex CO5 9PG. 01376 570000 www.kingsseeds.com

The Garlic Farm, Mersley Lane, Newchurch, Isle of Wight PO36 0NP. 01983 865378 www.thegarlicfarm.co.uk.

The Organic Gardening Catalogue, Riverdene, Molesey Road, Hersham, Surrey KT12 4RG. Tel 0845 1301304 www.Organic-Catalogue.com.

Victoriana Nursery, Buck Street, Challock, Ashford, Kent TN5 4DG. 01233 740527 www.victoriananursery.co.uk.

Access Garden Products, Yelvertoft Road, Crick, Northampton NN6 7XS. 01788 823811 www.garden-products.co.uk.

Harrod Horticultural, Pinbush Road, Lowestoft, Suffolk NR33 7NL. 0845 218 5301 www.harrodhorticultural.com.

Wiggly Wigglers, Lower Blakemere Farm, Blakemere, Herefordshire HR2 9PX. 01981 500391. www.wigglywigglers.co.uk.

Garden Organic, Ryton-on-Dunsmore, Coventry, Warwickshire CV8 3LG 024 7630 351 www.gardenorganic.org.uk (including the Heritage Seed Library)

Royal Horticultural Society (RHS), 80 Vincent Square, London, SW1P 2PE. 0845 2605000 www.rhs.org.

Some Useful Websites and Forums
www.homefarmer.co.uk
www.homesweethomefront.co.uk
www.allotment.org.uk
www.realgardeners.co.uk
www.rhs.org.uk
www.foodupfront.org
www.allotments4all.co.uk

Food up Front is an organisation dedicated to getting as many people in urban areas as possible growing veg.

Flowerpot Farming

Life Expectancy of Saved Seed

(These timescales refer to those seeds harvested directly from your own plants, or in the case of shop-bought seed packets, once the foil inner sachet, if there is one, has been opened. Factory sealed foil sachets will keep for much longer; the expiry date on the seed packet will advise.)

Bean, Broad	2 years
Bean, French	2 years
Bean, Runner	2 years
Beetroot	2 years
Beet, Leaf	2 years
Broccoli, Sprouting	3 years
Brussels Sprouts	4 years
Cabbage, green or red	3 years
Cabbage, Savoy	5 years
Carrot	4 years
Cauliflower	3 years
Celeriac	4 years
Cucumber, outdoor	6 years
Kale	4 years
Kohl Rabi	4 years
Leek	4 years
Lettuce	3 years
Marrow/Courgette	6 years
Onion (seed, not sets)	1-2 years
Parsnip	1 year
Peas	2 years
Peppers	5 years
Pumpkin/Squash	6 years
Radish	4 years
Spinach, annual	2 years
Sweet corn	2 years
Swiss Chard	2 years
Tomatoes, outdoor	3 years
Turnips	2 years

Glossary of Common Gardening Terms

Acid Soil | Soils with little or no traces of lime are described as 'acid'. Improvements can be made by adding lime, but be careful not to overdo it or, alternatively, consult an expert.

Alkaline soil | This is soil containing varying degrees of lime. Much less common than acid soil. Adding organic matter will help to improve it.

Annual | A fast-growing plant with a total lifespan of only one season, i.e. lettuce, basil. Most vegetables are treated as annuals, sown in spring and harvested later the same year.

Aphid | Tiny insects which are a common pest of many plants. As well as leaving a honeydew residue, particularly on new shoots, aphids are major carriers of viral diseases. Small infestations can be dealt with by squashing by hand, or sprayed with a mild detergent mixed with water.

Biennial | Plants that survive for two years, being sown one year to crop the next.

Blanching | Process carried out to whiten the stems of vegetables such as celery, leeks and chicory by excluding light.

Blight | A major airborne viral disease of potatoes and tomatoes. Worse in damp, humid summers.

Bolting | ('running to seed') Premature flowering caused by hot, dry conditions. Lettuce and spinach are particularly prone, but the stress caused by these conditions can affect many types of vegetable.

Bottom heat | A gentle source of heat supplied by propagators or heated mats. Assists greatly in developing seedling and root growth.

Catch crop | A quick growing crop planted on soil where a slower growing crop will be planted later in the year. Makes good use of limited space. Ideal vegetables: radish, turnip, rocket, pak-choi.

Certified Stock | Stock guaranteed free of infection and diseases, ie. certified seed potatoes.

Flowerpot Farming

Chitting | Starting tubers or seed ready for planting or sowing. Encourages growth of sprouts on potato tubers.

Compost | Planting/sowing medium, either proprietary bought pre-packed (multi-purpose, seed, potting, etc.) or homemade from varying mixtures of mainly decomposed vegetable matter, soil and small amounts of animal manure.

Cordon | Fruit tree or vegetable plant which has been trained or pruned back to a single upright stem.

Crocks | Broken clay pots used in the bottom of containers to help drainage. Large stones are a good alternative.

Crop rotation | A system of growing which ensures members of the same crop family are not grown in the same place year after year, preventing disease build up and nutrient depletion. A three or four year rotation is generally agreed to be effective.

Cross-pollination | Some fruit trees need other varieties in order to pollinate them to produce crops.

Crown | Part of a fruit or vegetable that is underground, normally the growing point from which leaves or shoots emerge, for example rhubarb and asparagus.

Curcurbits | Members of the marrow family: courgettes, squash and pumpkins.

Determinate | Bush habit. In tomatoes, the opposite of cordons. Plants are left unpruned, to produce side shoots.

Die-back | Caused by fungal disease - stems die back, starting from the growing tips. Affected parts should be pruned back to healthy growth.

Dormant | Inactive state of a plant in winter (e.g. fruit trees). This is the best time to prune.

Drill | A narrow furrow in soil into which seeds are sown.

Earthing up | Pulling up soil around plants such as potatoes (to prevent 'green' potatoes) and celery (to blanch).

156

F1 hybrid | Type of seed which produces crops of consistent quality, size and vigour. More expensive than normal 'open pollinated' seed, it is produced by crossing two pure bred strains by hand. Seed from F1 hybrid plants will not breed true, and so seed saving is not viable.

Fertilizer | Either natural organic material or manufactured substances incorporated into soil to improve fertility and yields.

Foliar feeding | Method of directing liquid feeds onto plants by applying to the leaves by spraying.

Half hardy | Plants that can be grown outside in the summer, but are not frost hardy.

Hardy | Term used for plants that can be grown outside all year round.

Haulm | The growing parts (stems, leaves) of crops such as potatoes and peas which die off after harvest.

Humus | Important element found in soil which is produced by the decomposition of organic matter. Humus affects the soil consistency and water holding abilities.

Indeterminate | Stems that grow indefinitely: eg. tomatoes and runner beans. Growth can be stopped once the plant has reached its desired height by pinching out the top.

Legume | Members of the pea and bean family – those crops producing pods.

Liquid manure | Natural liquid fertilizer from either animal manure or plant materials.

Loam | Term used to describe a well balanced soil, rich in humus.

Maiden | A young, first year fruit tree.

Mildew | White, powdery fungus caused by damp conditions and bad ventilation.

Mulch | A top dressing of organic materials, normally applied to suppress weed growth, lock in moisture and add nutrients to the soil.

Flowerpot Farming

Neutral soil | pH7 – soil that is neither acid nor limey (alkaline).

NPK | Abbreviation used for the three main plant foods – N for nitrogen (leaf growth), P for phosphorus (roots) and K for potassium (fruit and flowers).

Perennial | Plants that live for more than 2 years are described as perennials. Many carry foliage and stems which die completely over the winter but re-grow in spring.

Perlite | Small, white granules made from volcanic rock. Often mixed into compost to aid aeration and moisture retention.

Perpetual | Crops with long harvesting period, i.e. perpetual spinach.

Pot bound/root bound | Plant that has outgrown its pot and whose roots have no more room to grow. Vegetables should never be allowed to reach this state as it will negatively affect yields. Some container fruit trees, however, produce better crops when their roots are restricted.

Potting on | Re-potting a plant that has outgrown its pot to a large one with a larger soil/root capacity.

Pricking out | The process of transplanting seedlings from their seed trays into their final, or larger containers.

Propagator | A heated, covered tray used for raising seed and cuttings.

Raised bed | A bed filled with soil held in place with a retaining structure. Extends the growing depth when placed over existing soil at ground level.

Rootstock | Lower section of fruit tree, including roots, onto which a named variety is grafted to increase fruit yields.

Rose | Spray head of a watering can or hose.

Runner | Shoots sent out from parent plants from which roots and new plants develop (eg. strawberry runners).

Seed leaf | First one or pair of leaves to emerge from germinating seed. These do not usually resemble the adult or 'true' leaves.

Glossary

Seedling | Newly emerged young plant.

Soft fruit | Fruit other than tree (top) fruit, produced on bushes or on canes, eg. gooseberries and raspberries.

Soil testing | Simple soil testing kits analyse the pH of the soil and can be bought from garden centres.

Subsoil | Second layer of soil underneath the topsoil. Contains little or no nutrients.

Successional Sowing | Sowing vegetable seed at regular intervals is very useful for fast growing varieties. Small quantities of vegetables such as lettuce and radish sown regularly should provide manageable yields.

Tender | Not frost hardy.

Thinning | Removing some seedlings in order to provide more space for those remaining to develop to maturity.

Tilth | A fine, workable layer of soil.

Top dressing | Spreading fertilizer onto the soil surface around plants without digging in.

Top soil | Surface layer of soil containing nutrients and organic matter.

Transplant | Re-establishing a plant from one place to another.

True leaves | Adult, mature plant leaves.

The Good Life Press Ltd.
PO Box 536
Preston
PR2 9ZY
01772 652693

The Good Life Press publishes a wide range of titles for the smallholder, farmer and country dweller as well as Home Farmer, the monthly magazine aimed at anyone who wants to grab a slice of the good life - whether they live in the country or the city.

Other titles of interest

A Guide to Traditional Pig Keeping by Carol Harris
An Introduction to Keeping Cattle by Peter King
An Introduction to Keeping Sheep by J Upton/D Soden
Build It! by Joe Jacobs
Cider Making by Andrew Lea
First Find a Field by Rosamund Young
Grow and Cook by Brian Tucker
How to Butcher Livestock and Game by Paul Peacock
Making Jams and Preserves by Diana Sutton
Precycle! by Paul Peacock
Showing Sheep by Sue Kendrick
Talking Sheepdogs by Derek Scrimgeour
The Bread and Butter Book by Diana Sutton
The Cheese Making Book By Paul Peacock
The Pocket Guide to Wild Food by Paul Peacock
The Polytunnel Companion by Jayne Neville
The Sausage Book by Paul Peacock
The Shepherd's Companion by Jane Upton
The Smoking and Curing Book by Paul Peacock
The Urban Farmer's Handbook by Paul Peacock

www.goodlifepress.co.uk
www.homefarmer.co.uk